BABY

C000022426

Jason Davis was born in Adelaide in 1971 and has continued his good form ever since. After escaping Mullumbimby High School in 1988 during particularly rowdy bicentennial celebrations, Jason spent five years in the Royal Australian Air Force before scouring the country for a career that centred on the judicious use of fart jokes. He found it at *Australian Mad* magazine, which led to non-flatulence-related work at magazines and newspapers including the Qantas inflight magazine, the *Sydney Morning Herald*, the *Sun-Herald* and the *Courier-Mail*. Jason lives in Brisbane with his family and tries to keep out of harm's way.

BABY STEPS

A Bloke's-Eye View of IVF

Jason Davis

ALLEN&UNWIN

First published in 2006

Copyright © Jason Davis 2006

All rights reserved. No part of this book may be reproduced or transmitted in any form or by any means, electronic or mechanical, including photocopying, recording or by any information storage and retrieval system, without prior permission in writing from the publisher. The *Australian Copyright Act 1968* (the Act) allows a maximum of one chapter or 10 per cent of this book, whichever is the greater, to be photocopied by any educational institution for its educational purposes provided that the educational institution (or body that administers it) has given a remuneration notice to Copyright Agency Limited (CAL) under the Act.

Allen & Unwin
83 Alexander Street
Crows Nest NSW 2065
Australia
Phone: (61 2) 8425 0100
Fax: (61 2) 9906 2218
Email: info@allenandunwin.com
Web: www.allenandunwin.com

National Library of Australia
Cataloguing-in-Publication entry:

Davis, Jason, 1971- .
   Baby steps : a bloke's-eye view of IVF.

   ISBN 1 74114 740 9.

   1. Fertilization in vitro, Human - Australia.   2.
   Infertility, Male.   3. Infertility - Treatment - Australia.
   I. Title.

618.1780599

Set in 12/16 pt Rotis Serif by Bookhouse, Sydney
Printed in Australia by McPherson's Printing Group

10 9 8 7 6 5 4 3 2 1

CONTENTS

PREFACE

This is a personal story. It chronicles Liz and my white-knuckled ride strapped onto the clunky, well-worn metaphor that is the IVF rollercoaster. As any fertility specialist worth their progesterone will tell their patients, every cycle of IVF (or similar procedure) is unique. As such, this book does not set out to be a textbook or a definitive guide to the process, merely an extra piece of ammunition (and another dodgy metaphor) for couples to take into the IVF battle. In short, I tried to write the book that I wish we had read before we hit the frontlines. While the news from our pants continued to be disheartening, Liz and I always found it a great relief and a bit of a surprise to discover that we were not alone in our predicament. Ours is only one of thousands of stories from thousands of couples who have endured the IVF process.

Had we known then what we know now, would we still have done it? Of course. As the many thousands of

IVF parents around the country will tell you, there ain't no mountain high enough.

I would like to thank the following people for their help in producing this book: Dr Robert Watson for his medical expertise, grace and good humour, Colette Vella for her eagle eye and Jo Paul for the quickest green light in the business. Their help was invaluable but any errors are mine alone. Thanks are also due to Kirsten Galliott, Ronnie Gramazio and Lesley McFadzean, without whom this book would not exist.

I also thank Bart, Glen, Dave, Helen and Alana for being there when I needed them.

This book is dedicated to my wife Elizabeth, without whom the volume before you—and my life, I suspect— would be a sad little affair. Why she married me I have yet to comprehend, although I now suspect a voodoo curse is involved.

GOOD EVENING, LADIES AND SPERMS . . .

You wouldn't notice the doorway unless you had business inside. I'd lived in the next suburb for two years and never seen it standing there in wait, sandwiched discreetly between a travel agent and a place that sold designer bathroom fixtures. I wasn't expecting a flashing neon arrow, heaven forbid, but the door was obviously designed to blend in—plain and grey and recessed into the space between shopfronts with only an ambiguous Mayne sign hanging from the awning to give it away.

No, only those with pathology lab business would give it a second thought—doctors, couriers, lab staff and, of course, skittish men carrying warm jars of their own semen.

Early on that hot weekday morning in January 2003, I found myself rushing along the main street of Sydney's

Little Italy with a paper bag in my hand and a *Mission: Impossible* timer ticking in my head. My mission—and I had already accepted it—was to get my sperm sample into the hands of the lab boffins within 45 minutes, before my swimmers stopped doing laps and self-destructed.

Around me, the inner-west suburb of Leichhardt was starting to come to life and get where it needed to go before the day turned into a real stinker. Espresso machines gargled, flowers were placed in buckets of water and lines were forming at the bakery for the day's fresh ciabatta. Among the Latin gesturing and small-business hubbub, I hurried on.

Liz and I had been married for sixteen months, and after nine months of officially sanctioned 'trying' for a baby there had been no sign that my sperm or her eggs were even on nodding terms. Things weren't quite going to plan, so we resolved to 'get checked out' as the euphemism goes. Once the decision was made, I consigned it to the too-hard basket while she conscientiously made appointments, gained referrals and before I knew it was two months along her road of reproductive discovery. I dragged the chain for as long as I could, but eventually found myself in front of a quack, who furnished me with a plastic jar and a paper bag and sent me on my way.

So there I was at the door to Mayne Pathology. For an instant I expected it to be locked, but it swung open easily and I entered with the confidence of a man who had just had one off the wrist and felt the need to show complete strangers the results.

Inside, it was still 1986. The lab reception area reminded me of one of those side-street hairdressing salons that time forgot, but in place of a glowing scissors steriliser and faded posters of men with undulating New Romantic coifs were yellowing health posters, a stunted happy plant in a plastic pot and an unmanned front desk. The actual analysis of samples obviously took place in the rear of the establishment and that was where I tried to direct my frantic pinging of the reception bell. In 3.4 seconds I'd read all about CPR, chlamydia and the safe disposal of sharps and was hopping from foot to foot, trying to guess what the three old men sitting along one wall were doing there. Maybe they had a three-for-one coupon for a colon scraping and were waiting for their results sheet. Whoever they were, they had no qualms in staring unashamedly at the only thing of interest in the room—me.

Just when I'd steeled myself to perform CPR on each and every one of my sperm, a large woman with even larger hair appeared and gently removed the bell from my reach.

I thrust my bag forward. 'My surname is Davis...a sample...'

'Put your name, date and time of collection on it, have you?' she bellowed. It was a voice that would have put Pavarotti to shame.

Before I could answer, she ripped the jar from its paper bag and considered it thoughtfully. Then, with a puzzled look, she gave the jar a shake and held it up to the fluorescent light. Four pairs of eyes followed it skyward while I concentrated on counting the constituent molecules of the floor tiles.

I can confidently say that a single volume-related wisecrack at that moment would have seen me spontaneously combust with embarrassment. Happily, the Maria Venuti of sperm analysis said nothing, content to roll my seed around and frown for several more excruciating seconds.

I'm the first to admit that there were no volume records broken in the completion of my ejaculatory obligation but, in my defence, juggling a jar and your knob while having a wank in the spare bedroom with one eye on the clock to make sure you rendezvous with the 8.03 bus to the city does take some of the excitement out of the process.

Mercifully, I was soon dismissed and I very nearly knocked Maria over in my hurry to slam the door on the rheumy stares of the Brothers Grim. Unfortunately I skidded to a stop on the pavement outside only to discover that the bus stop across the street was packed with Catholic schoolgirls. Now, I've caught enough public transport to know that giggling and behind-the-hand whispering are the two favourite pastimes of any brand of schoolgirl, but was it my imagination or had all eyes at this bus stop just turned to the slamming door across the road?

Liz and I pretty much knew from the word go that we both wanted children. I think we knew this before we even formally discussed it. I assume we subconsciously felt each other out—even before we felt each other up—

the way people do when they start to go out, searching for major ideological mismatches, incompatible fetishes or large caches of Nana Mouskouri albums.

This process started on our first date, a momentous occasion for which I was very keen, quite late, and wearing wet pants.

Allow me to explain.

I was 28 and living alone in Randwick, in Sydney's east, in a one-bedroom flat. I was a fairly normal single guy—think Tintin, without the plus-fours, exciting international adventures and little white dog. As a homeowner and enlightened male-type person, I had become reasonably domesticated and, it being 1999, I'd had the best part of a decade to absorb the occasional SNAGish tip for interacting with womenfolk. To make a good impression, I'd shelled out for a new shirt for the big date and even tossed my good jeans in the wash. God, I must have been keen.

As the sun set on that Saturday, I ventured out to the line only to find that an afternoon's sunshine had done little to dry my soggy strides. What's worse, half an hour of frantic ironing made only a vague impression on the damp denim. Clearly, the more I ironed, the later I was going to be, so I was faced with the question that has dogged mankind throughout the ages: what is more important, punctuality or dry pants? By the time I chafed my way into the Clock Hotel in Surry Hills and sat down, I was both steaming at the groin and twenty minutes late.

But it didn't matter. Sitting at a table by herself was Elizabeth Herron, 26, absolutely radiant. I remember her there positioned in the centre of a spotlight, but that has to be a trick of memory. She was so beautiful I literally could not look her in the eye. Initially I sat across from her, examining my hands, the wall, the tabletop, trying to act natural so as not to appear out of my league but wanting to attract attention to us at the same time. After all, it wasn't often I found myself out on the town with a vision of this calibre—a woman capable of eliciting envious looks from other blokes. It was almost like I wanted confirmation that it was actually happening.

The sheer relief at finally getting there had me babbling like an idiot. In the half-hour we stayed before leaving for the restaurant, I think she knew more about me than was either wise or healthy at that point. If I'd thought about it at all, rather than being mesmerised by my own good fortune, I would have played it cooler. Who am I kidding—cool is not my strong suit. I'm more of a specialist in fool.

One Indian banquet later and cool was even further off the agenda. It was one of the greatest feelings of my life.

We'd agreed that Liz would be in charge of the after-dinner entertainment and she'd decided on the Sounds of Seduction 60s retro night at the Lansdowne Hotel, just out of the CBD at Broadway. Eeeeexcellent. She was playing right into my hands.

Go-go dancers, lava lamps and beanbags I was prepared for, but the Russ Meyer clips projected onto the walls took us both by surprise. Which one of his highbrow epics we were watching I couldn't say, but *Pandora's Peaks* certainly figured prominently in the mix. Projected

10-feet tall on the wall, there was enough light coming off those big white boobs to read the drinks menu by. I remember spending the best part of an hour dutifully looking anywhere but at the Meyer-fest before us and protesting that I couldn't believe they would show that kind of stuff. Liz told me to shut up and dragged me onto the dance floor.

We fell out of the place at around three and the evening culminated in a romantic stroll along Parramatta Road—just the carbon monoxide, cruising V8s and us. Being the king of romance that I am, at one point I followed a hunch and dragged my date into a boarded-up doorway and had the snog of my life.

And the best part? It was the snog of her life too.

A year later, we were house-hunting.

The commute between Liz's job in western Sydney and me in the east had quickly lost its novelty value for Liz, who was doing most of the actual commuting. I had sold my flat a few months earlier after evil neighbours had hijacked my cat by feeding him chicken breast and fillet steak and adopted him out from under me. I was far too mad to stay, so I sold up and moved in with a mate in nearby Coogee. It was an ideal batch pad near the beach—full of sand, empty pizza boxes and bizarre fungus-based life forms growing in the bottom of the fridge—but it was even further from Drummoyne and The Lovely Liz, as she was now universally known.

Something had to give, and Sydney's relentless traffic had the final say.

With two steady incomes behind us and the proceeds from the sale of my flat and my car, we pulled out the calculator and discovered that if we tightened our belts a notch we could just afford to buy one of the finest undercover parking spaces in the entire eastern suburbs. But Liz seemed stuck on the idea of bedrooms and a backyard, so we struck out further afield, and started hunting for a 'handyman's delight' in the inner west. I figured all I'd have to do was kidnap a handyman and we'd be in business.

Although Liz informs me we only looked for a month, the auctions and inspection-infested Saturdays from that and other house-hunting stints have blurred together in my brain to form a kind of numbing property twilight. I remember inspections and disappointments and the ritual humiliation of real estate snakes downplaying values to get us to auctions for the privilege of witnessing the first bid bust our upper-upper-stretch-a-bit-too-far limit. Gearing up for another such auction emasculation, we'd decided to do a quick inspection at a tiny cottage on an anorexic sliver of land in Lilyfield.

O'Neill Street was a nice spot. It was leafy, relatively quiet when the passenger aircraft weren't threatening to touch down on the roof, nice and wide and only a stone's throw to a very big park. Sure, the park used to be a mental hospital and there was still one high-security ward there, but we'd been on the hunt long enough to know that these kinds of facts are considered semantics in the world of real estate.

We got there before the agent, a flustered, bumbling sort of fellow who knew less about the property than we did. He had recently struck out on his own to form a small agency and the workload was clearly dragging him and his hairline into a premature middle age. He finally found a key that worked and flung the door open for us.

Oh boy.

Among the house's major downfalls were, in no particular order, the rusty tin roof, dodgy guttering, up-and-down borer-riddled floorboards, the rotten and precarious fences and carport, and the Leaning Tower of Besser blocks retaining wall in the backyard. The living-room floor was matted rental carpet over chipboard, the two substances fused together through a combination of mould and extreme foot traffic, and the kitchen was a lime-green Laminex 1970s special.

It was ours by the end of the week.

It was all Liz's idea. Our general property inspection modus operandi was to give as little away as possible until we had a chance to confer on the walk back to the car, and O'Neill Street was no exception. The conversation went something like this:

Me (holding nose): 'Peee-ew. That's a big "no way" on that stinker. Where's the nearest pub around here anyway?'

Liz: 'Really? I thought it was pretty decent. You could do a lot with it.'

And so it went. My brilliant, big-picture girlfriend saw the place's potential: new floorboards here, a lick of paint and a half-kilo of plastique there. As a single-fronted cottage on a slice of land a mere 4.8 metres wide, what it had in abundance was cosiness. This is not difficult when you can reach out and touch both outer walls at once, but the cosy cottage feel counts for a lot. So we sold everything of any value we had accumulated during our entire lives and signed over legal custody of our souls to the bank.

For us new cohabitants, the last six months of the millennium was all about coats of paint, throw rugs and flat-pack furniture. We were nesting. Liz surrounded herself in paint chips, I owned my first garden shed and we were actually getting along, living together, making a home.

That's not to say there wasn't some adjusting going on. Liz was conscious of giving me a bit of space and I was conscious of not prompting the person who prepared most of the meals to reach for the Ratsak.

Things were travelling so well that we soon felt the need to complicate matters with a pair of surrogate children.

From the depressingly abundant stocks at the Animal Welfare League we plucked a street pup, a black-and-tan poodle cross who'd been found abandoned and malnourished. He would need a nice solid name in case the other puppies thought he was French or an interior designer, so we named him Bob. To keep him in line, at the RSPCA we discovered Matilda, a tiny black terrier cross with a tan face and comical John Howard-esque eyebrows—part gremlin, part Hairy Maclary, and maybe just a smattering of muskrat.

We had the house and the dogs, as tiny and warped as they all were. There could be only one thing next on the agenda.

●

The dual meaning of the word virile is a good example of how society subtly teaches men to rate themselves. 'Virile' means 'potent' but its secondary meaning is 'attractive' or 'manly', probably stemming from ye olde medieval days when the main criterion for women selecting a bloke was to find someone of good genetic stock who could help you pump out at least a half-dozen kiddies. This would help ensure the bloodline had the best chance of prospering.

In more modern culture, the double meaning still exists. How many times in old movies have we heard the screen siren pant 'Oooh, you're so virile' when the hero of the piece eventually talks her into bed. In the male psyche, if a man can't get his wife pregnant, then he's barely worthy of the title, let alone a second glance, right? Would Liz look at me differently now? Should I put my blank-firing pistol back in the holster and step aside so she could make a life with someone with live ammunition? Women could get a pill for their problems, but where was mine? I oscillated between anger, listlessness and frustration.

And yet somehow time passed and the sky did not fall in. Liz, in a supreme test of her compassionate nature and persistence, even managed to get me to talk through some of my frustration. It was good to chat, but the reality of the situation was slowly hitting home.

We were officially one of those couples 'having trouble', and it was probably my fault.

SATURDAY NIGHT'S A FIGHT, ALL RIGHT

Asking a journalist to give up coffee and alcohol is like asking him to give up breathing. And bitching about the government. And turning up to work drunk.

A few months into our reproductive investigations, we had been told by a series of doctors to clean up our acts, diet-wise, if we were serious about falling pregnant. We were deadly serious, so our diets were about to become deadly dull.

The collective do's and don'ts as advised by our doctors, a raft of self-help books and bales of pseudo-helpful fact sheets included:

- Don't drink alcohol.
- Give up both coffee and tea.

The spectre of marriage was soon to raise its head, check its pocketwatch and call 'time please'.

Liz had, in no uncertain terms, ensured my intentions were long term when she fused her finances with mine in buying the house. I think the phrase 'it needn't happen overnight, but it will happen' figured prominently in the conversation, and we weren't talking hair care. But she had no reason to worry; I felt the same. I'd already told Liz I wanted to spend the rest of my life with her and I meant it.

Since I began to realise that I wasn't going to be in short pants my whole life, I had always seen myself becoming a father one day. During my childhood and into my adolescence, this notion crystallised from a vague aspiration into the desire for the ultimate familial cliché. When I imagined what it would be like to be a father, to really feel like the cornerstone of a family, I saw a scene straight out of Hollywood, one where I would arrive home after a hard day at work, drive past the white picket fence and park in the driveway of my handsome family home and be greeted by the loving wife and 2.4 kids rushing across the manicured lawn and into my arms. Sometimes there were two kids, sometimes four, but there was always green grass, white pickets and even whiter smiles.

If I had the time or the inclination, I could probably identify many of the 70s and 80s movies and sitcoms that lodged in my brain to form this TV amalgam, but it doesn't really matter. It was my Everest, and it loomed so large over me because of the perspective on fatherhood I had gained as a boy.

My father had left my mother and me when I was about two years old. In later years, after I stopped seeing life as quite such a black and white affair, I asked Mum why they had split, and the answer was a mundane one. They had married too young and had wanted different things out of life, so he left and stayed away. When my mother remarried, as a six-year-old it took me a while to warm to my new stepfather, and when their marriage ended badly, I found myself bitter and even more confused about my place in the world and what fatherhood was. I have no doubt this instability at crucial times in my upbringing fast-tracked the formation of my fantasy family and steeled my resolve to be a dad. But not just any dad— a great dad. A better dad than mine had been to me.

Now I had met The Lovely Liz, fatherhood wasn't so far-fetched after all. I loved her, we both wanted kids, and the woman was under the illusion I was a catch, so I needed to stitch up the deal quickly, before she sobered up, or the gypsy hex on her was lifted. Marriage was on the agenda. It was just a question of when.

The polite inquiries from family and friends started when we moved in together and were gathering intensity. Little did they know that the wheels were already in motion—tracking through the dew on a golf course, where many manly D&Ms take place.

My best mate Derek and I played a lot of early-morning golf in those days. Shivering on the first tee before the sun had penetrated the deep hills of the Lane

Cove course, many was the day I would slice my ball down a ravine, turn to him and casually ask, 'So, with this rest of your life stuff, when do you reckon you really *know*?' Over hundreds of holes, bacon-and-egg rolls and more than a few breakfast beers, I realised that the well-muscled arm of God was never going to reach down and anoint me as ready. I was going to have to go with my gut, and with a couple of beers rolling around in it, my gut seemed like it knew what it was doing.

In October 2000, Sydney's Level 41 (or just 41 for those on nodding terms with the maître d') was the pinnacle of fine dining, at least in my eyes. I'd heard the food was first-rate and the views from the urinal unsurpassed, and I do like a nice bathroom. It would be the venue for my Decent Proposal.

The restaurant was suitably opulent, and we were served drinks in the lounge on arrival. Liz looked resplendent as usual in a strappy number, but I wouldn't have been less comfortable had my genitalia been a menu item. I struggle with nerves under pressure, always have, and I knew that if I didn't pop the question before dinner I'd be too sick to eat and would miss what would be the meal of the year—and sweating into the starter would give the game away anyway, so I took a deep breath, pushed my seat back, got down on bended knee and asked Elizabeth if she would be my wife. It is one of the few times I can remember calling her Elizabeth when she wasn't in trouble.

With tears welling and face flushed, she said yes. The expensive vino had been a wise investment.

What struck me most about the event, as much as the overwhelming blend of love, relief, pride and excitement, and the shimmering Sydney cityscape, was the reaction of the other diners. We were one of the tables closest to the view, so most of the other tables looked onto ours, and it was so quiet you could have heard a cotton ball drop onto the tasteful carpet. Yet when I got out of my seat and asked Elizabeth 'to do me the honour of becoming my wife' did they cheer, did they clap, did they stand and toast our happiness?

Not a peep.

We set the date for 30 September, and the year of leeway we'd allowed ourselves evaporated quickly. Liz began plotting and scheming with her mum and friends, and I—well, I knew a decent suit rental place, so I was pretty much sorted.

Not being avid churchgoers, we were planning a garden wedding, and we'd stumbled onto an historic little sandstone cottage among parklands on a point at Gladesville. They say it once belonged to Banjo Paterson, but I don't recall it featuring in any of his more famous poems, so this was never confirmed. But it really was a lovely spot, so we booked in. Before we knew it my mum and Pommy uncles were flying in and friends from interstate were booking hotel rooms. I was about to step into the lead role in *2001: A Marriage Odyssey*.

A week of rain had given way to a glorious day, all blue skies, bees and warm spring breezes and, as the sun slowly sank, friends, family, a string quartet and our zany house-painter-turned-ship's-captain-turned-celebrant gathered at the cottage restaurant for our sunset wedding. We later learned that our celebrant (who would have performed the ceremony dressed as Elvis for an extra $100) somehow managed to jam his accelerator to the floor while driving to the venue. He made the trip screaming up to each set of traffic lights, knocking the car out of gear and jumping on the brake, only to burn rubber from a standing start again. This was par for the course for him. I consider it a win that he didn't turn up on a pogo stick.

But minor hiccups aside, it was a glorious night.

We exchanged our vows in front of friends and family as the sun set on the lush garden and the yachts poodled home on the surrounding waterways. Far from the bundle of nerves I'd been all afternoon, as soon as my vows left my lips, everything felt right. It was a great moment. Mums misted up, grandparents sat and squeezed each other's hands and loved ones stood around sipping bubbly and smiling at the scene. I was grinning fit to burst.

Soon we were inside tucking in to a brilliant meal, availing ourselves of the open bar, and warming the dance floor.

Amid all the festivities I recall looking at my reflection in the bathroom and wondering at the source of my dumb luck. Beautiful wife, house, decent job, great dogs, nice family, good health. Life was ticking along just fine, thank you very much.

Few things have the potential to knock a man off his perch faster than the results of a sperm test.

In January 2003, a few days after taking my taddies on a whistlestop tour of the inner west, I had myself another appointment with my GP. I took a seat in his room and after a minute he looked up from scribbling on papers strewn across his desk. For him, just another day of medicine; for me, a day of reckoning. This was the moment where my manhood would either be confirmed, allowing me to resume breathing, or destroyed, ensuring my ego cowboy would forever shoot blanks.

The doc put down his pen and picked up my file. 'Okay, Mr... Davis. Now, you're my... ah yes, semen analysis.'

'Mmmfr.' Somehow my mouth was full of glue but my bowels were sliding around on castors.

'I've got the result sheet here, so let's have a look. Did you say last time that you've been trying for a baby?'

'That's right. We've been at it for... maybe nine months.'

The clock ticked. He scanned the page in front of him. Somewhere an air-conditioner hummed.

'Right.'

A beat. Then many more.

What was taking so long? Why was he scowling like that? Were the figures so low they were printed in a reduced font size? Were there tiny sketches of the individual sperm at the bottom of the page? I strained to pick numerals out of the inverted jumble of text, but it was no good.

'So... do you know about the four main numbers we quote in sperm analysis? There is the volume of semen produced; the actual sperm count within that; motility, which is how many are swimming forward, if you like; and morphology, which is how many look to be formed correctly.'

'Okay.'

'First of all, volume. The normal range of semen produced is greater than 2 millilitres. You produced 2.2...'

Is it inappropriate to high-five during a sperm briefing? I swear if he'd stuck his hand up I would have slapped the fingernails off it. Under ideal conditions—preferably without a small plastic jar involved—who knows the voluminous outpourings I could achieve!

'... which is a little low, but within limits. Then there is the sperm count or sperm concentration—probably the most important number. We say the normal range is greater than 20 million per millilitre. I'm afraid you've tested at just 15 million, which is quite low.'

The honky-tonk pianist froze, the record stylus was ripped across the LP and in a bar somewhere someone dropped a tray of glasses. I don't remember the other two figures—I was devoting all my cranial resources to remembering how to breathe.

I took some personal time, then unlocked my jaw. 'That's still 15 million of the little fellas on my side, right?'

The kindly doctor with the white hair removed his glasses and smiled. 'It is, but with such a long fight ahead of them, you really need more troops than that.'

'Right.'

'I think you might have to get used to the idea that you may never have children.'

SHACKING UP IS HARD TO DO

Ah, wedded bliss. The ring on my finger had magically made the sun shine just that little bit brighter, the flowers bloom in hues a shade more intense, and the siren call of the seafood buffet just that bit more insistent. Three days in, ensconced on a tropical island in the Whitsundays with a pina colada in each hand, counting the hours until the dinnertime mêlée, I was my own Lord of the Ring. Marriage was looking like a pretty good deal.

Post-honeymoon, we had arrived home relaxed, tanned and more than a little contented calorie-wise, and settled into the well-worn routine. Weekdays were for work, dog walks and the odd dinner out; weekends were spent socialising, on more dog walks and trying to find our way out of Ikea. Nothing should have changed, and yet something seemed subtly different.

Over the next few months the post-wedding glow wore off and exposed an insidious undercurrent of disquiet slithering along beneath it.

There was griping. We started picking. Where we would happily cede ground and laugh off disagreements as 'boyfriend and girlfriend' now we were prepared to go toe to toe to argue the toss. We were suddenly arguing like, well, like people who had been married for much longer, and we didn't know why. And we are talking about complete trivialities here.

Me: 'Why must you persist in squeezing the toothpaste tube in the middle? You know it drives me spare.'

She: 'Actually, there's a scientific reason for it. Why don't you look it up for yourself in *The Big Book of Get A Life You Absolute Control Freak.* You don't seem to give a shit what I want when you wipe the benchtops with the sponge and leave it encrusted with filth.'

And so on.

These were not our exact words. When I sat down and tried to think of the arguments we had, I couldn't dredge up a single one, and that's kind of the point. We have subsequently polled friends and family and found this phenomenon to be relatively common among the newly hitched. I have a theory about it. I call it the Oh Shit, My Ejector Seat Is Missing, or OSMESIM hypothesis.

No, it's not Robert Ludlum's latest thriller from the grave. It's about the removal of the 'easy out' once the ceremony is over and the confetti hits the ground. I'm no psychologist, but I'm convinced that, subconsciously, when you know that you can't easily ditch the relationship when the going gets tough like you could have as a singleton, the mental defence mechanisms start to kick in. I know that Liz and I were the same people having the same good times in the same relationship two weeks either side of the wedding, but just try telling my subconscious that. The OSMESIM factor was lurking, waiting to jump us and crush the life out of our relationship. Even though in the eyes of the law we were de factos before our wedding—a legal state every bit as binding as marriage—after the ceremony the wedding rings start to feel a little bit weightier, about as heavy as a small ball and chain. If you remove the flight option from your primal 'fight or flight' mechanism, there are no prizes for guessing that you'll soon start wanting to protect yourself.

I blame fair maiden fairytales and bodice-ripper romance fiction. Too many women are counting on far too much from the male species and we're the first to admit that we're far from equipped to meet such lofty expectations.

Eventually, after many rivers of tears and countless hours of soul-searching, sleepless nights and diagram-drawing, we discovered the following salient points about ourselves and the opposing sex in general:

1. Women are indoctrinated into believing that once they are married, their lives will be filled with roses on pillows, romantic walks on the beach and that their ears will grow red and swollen with endless sweet-nothings whispering.
2. This is not possible.

3. Men believe that once they are married their lives will be exactly the same as when they were single, only with a woman around to have constant sex with them, strut around in lingerie and tell them how clever they are.

4. This is not possible.

5. When my wife complains that I make no special time for her and don't put her first, the time and energy taken in actually apologising and making a tiny, and possibly consistent effort to rectify this will be roughly one-tenth the time and energy spent trying to turn the blame on her and battling it out verbally.

6. If I handle No. 5 correctly, I will get much more back in return than I put in. If you know what I mean.

We unearthed these kernels of wisdom over the course of our first married year, and all it cost us was an almost constant succession of screaming fights, cold-shouldering and a two-way barrage of sledging and mental disintegration that Steve Waugh himself would have doffed his Baggy Green at.

One of the best fights happened on the great European tour of April and May 2002.

We'd planned a trip to the UK to witness my mate Derek marry his English fiancée May, and we stopped off for a ten-day pre-holiday holiday in España. Of the countries I've visited, if I was deported from Australia and forced to live overseas, I'd do a Chris Skase and make a beeline straight for Spain. (Hopefully it won't come to that, as long as certain people continue to keep their mouths shut. You know who you are.)

In true Spanish style, the argument erupted in the middle of the day, in the middle of the street.

After slightly overplanning the trip, I thought we'd wing it and book the last two nights in Madrid when we lobbed into town. Naturally the national societies of podiatrists, palaeontologists and prostate surgeons were all holding conferences in the city at the same time and there was nary a room to be found. After I'd been knocked back at a half-dozen of our initial choices, I left Liz and our backpacks sitting in a bar and took our Lonely Planet to a payphone to start inflicting my Spanish on the hoteliers on the remainder of the list. With my usual bravado, there is a chance I gave my wife the impression that I wouldn't be long, but not knowing how many calls it would take, or where the nearest payphone was (the one in the bar was out of order) I really had no clue.

It took roughly 60 calls in as many minutes to find us an overpriced room across the other side of town. Sometime between exhausting the first and second phone cards, my task turned into a quest, an odyssey that was to define my manhood, my very ability to overcome adversity and protect my mate. There also may have been some sunstroke involved.

So I returned to the bar expecting a hero's welcome—the great white hunter back from the wild veldt after securing shelter for the night. I was instead greeted by an irate wife who thought I had been abducted, jailed or at the very least mistaken for Tintin and mobbed by Belgians. She was furious, I was amazed, then confused, then furious in return, and we hoisted our packs and stormed out of the place spitting accusations at each other.

Outside, I'm not sure who started the screaming. Maybe it was me.

'Oh, okay! You'd prefer to sleep in the gutter than sit in a pub for an hour with a drink in your hand!? What fucking hardship you have endured. (To bystanders) Someone call the Red Cross!'

'Of course you couldn't manage to admit defeat just once and come back after ten minutes to let me know you were okay! Noooooo. We wouldn't dream of considering anyone else for a change, or that maybe I might be worried and maybe I didn't feel like sitting in a smoky bar on my own with a bunch of stinking Spaniards!'

By this stage we were on opposite footpaths bellowing broadsides across the street, and even the locals, to whom squabbling is a spectator sport, were wincing and ducking for cover. *¡Ay Caramba!*

The last thing I remember was each of us daring the other to 'fuck off in that direction', so God knows how we reunited and made it to the last hotel room in Madrid, and how we patched things up fast enough to ask for a *habitación matrimonio* (room with double bed) when we got there.

A few weeks later in the UK, after a lovely Somerset wedding, a trip north to substantially less lovely Newcastle to see my relatives and a drive back to London, we found ourselves in a $250-a-night fleabag room somewhere in central London. This was significant because, having just finished a cycle, Liz was off the pill for the first time in living memory.

It was to be the ultra-romantic site of our first attempt at becoming parents. I took my wife's hand, led her to the bed with the collapsed springs in the room with the paper-thin walls, drew the curtains on the procession of trucks rumbling by inches from our window and we made sweet love. Afterwards we fell asleep nose-to-nose on the concave bed dreaming of button-nosed kiddies with our features and chiropractors with the magic touch.

At home a fortnight later, Liz's period was late.

Could we have cracked it first try? Jesus, were we sure we were actually ready for parenthood for real? Liz's periods had always been spot-on for timing, but she had been on the pill for the better part of ten years.

It's all very well to plan these decisions, but I for one had mentally pencilled in a few months of diligent practice and unsuccessful attempts before we got it right. If it had happened first pop—well, it was just so *soon*, wasn't it.

Despite our reservations, there was a good deal of silent excitement going on at the time. You know, the kind when you might hold each other and jump up and down, but you do it quickly and quietly, as if too much jubilance will jinx it. We had whispered conversations about who would leave their job and counted ahead on our fingers to figure out what star sign the baby would be. For a few days I made my way through the world with a little secret—a little secret that never failed to make me smile.

It didn't last. Liz's period finally came about ten days late and our lives continued on regardless. It was no big deal, it was only our first try. We'd probably crack it next month.

It didn't happen. For seven months in a row it didn't happen, and Liz's period was late every time. For the majority of 2002 we found ourselves dashing up to the chemist for home pregnancy kits, each passing month bringing with it greater trepidation as she wizzed on the stick and showed me her handiwork. No matter how we squinted or held the stick on an angle, we could never quite conjure that elusive second red line.

We figured her cycle just needed a breather to recover from such a long stint on the pill and that it would correct itself over time, but the monkeys on our backs were gradually gaining weight and starting to hammer on their little brass alarm bells.

Then in October Liz's period had a holiday. It disappeared for two months and once again the stupid little stick could offer no good explanation. Had our circumstances been reversed, I would've followed the male form guide and consigned the situation to the medical 'too hard' basket but, to her credit, Liz was more proactive.

She had found a good female GP in Balmain who did a series of blood tests. Everything checked out okay, apart from a slightly elevated testosterone reading. On Liz's next visit, the GP told her about polycystic ovarian syndrome (PCOS), a condition that affects the normal function of the ovaries and results in their being covered in small cysts—hence the name. One of the symptoms of PCOS is elevated levels of testosterone. While it is normal for the female body to produce testosterone, PCOS can increase the hormone's production, which can lead to excessive hirsuteness, acne and obesity. An ultrasound was the only way to properly check her ovaries—PCOS would make them large and round, like golf balls, and the cysts on their surfaces would be visible. Liz duly booked herself in.

A few pamphlets and a session of internet surfing later and Liz was distraught. A little research is a dangerous thing. She was convinced that she was doomed to a life as an overweight, hairy, pimply-faced sasquatch-woman. Never mind that she actually exhibited none of these symptoms. Never mind that actually as many as one in five women (that ratio cheered her up for about fifteen seconds) *have* polycystic ovaries. Not all women who have polycystic ovaries exhibit the extra symptoms that push them into the 'syndrome' category, but it is a very common disease, the cause of which is unknown.

It took a while for the statistics to be of any comfort. Her femininity had taken a real body blow and it was up to me to heap on the positive reinforcement—an area of my brain that, to this day, remains puny and underdeveloped. I did my best and gradually her fragile self-image repaired itself. Living in the age of tell-all trash media helped the situation enormously—possibly the first time that sentence has ever applied in the history of tabloid journalism. We would be quietly enjoying some mind-numbing sitcom when Liz would burst forth with 'You know what I heard the other day!?'

'What's that?'

'You know Victoria Beckham? Apparently she has PCOS!'

'See? There you go. Now, isn't *The Simpsons* on?'

While Liz was starting on the long and painful road to medical self-discovery, I needed a project. The cynical amongst us would say that I was just casting about for a diversion because deep down I knew I should be getting checked out like my wife. I prefer to call it 'being handy'.

I began construction on The Great Wall of Lilyfield.

On the left side of our long sliver of a backyard, our neighbour's yard was about a metre higher than ours. On the boundary the previous owners of the house next door—I still think of them as slavering, zombie-like sub-humans—had built a 3-metre Besser block wall right on the edge of the drop-off. All that seemed to be stopping the wall toppling over onto our heads was a clump of invasive bamboo and the original rotten wooden boundary fence. The plan was to remove the bamboo and the rotten fence, carefully add concrete footings under the wall, and then build another low retaining wall the length of the main wall and join it to the main wall at the ends. I'd render the whole shebang with a sandstone finish and goodbye ugly Besser blocks, hello raised garden beds and central pond. Too easy.

We had no money for luxuries like getting building materials delivered, so I'd pack Liz's newish Lancer with bags of cement until it putted home resting on its springs.

I poisoned bamboo shoots and jackhammered off the old concrete squeezed between Besser blocks like Vegemite through a Vita-Weet. I hacked at the earth, mixed metres of concrete via barrow and spade, and watched large sheets of render languidly flop off the wall at my feet. I buried my head in the sand and cement while Liz soldiered on, facing an imminent attack on her femininity.

For Liz, the final step in her PCOS investigation involved a Christmas Eve encounter with a festively phallic ultrasound probe at an anonymous clinic in Newtown. For someone who still enjoys the tinsel and tradition of Christmas as much as my wife does, the timing of the appointment was particularly miserable. It was at about this point that Liz decided enough was enough; I too should be sashaying along the path of reproductive discovery. She impressed upon me that it was time I stopped arseing about and got to a doctor for a sperm test, to make sure that we didn't have a double problem on our hands. Holding the phone like it was contagious, I finally called for an appointment.

Sure enough, Liz's internal scan revealed two golf-ball-like ovaries covered in cysts that showed up as dark spots on the ultrasound. Her worst fear was confirmed, but her GP reassured her that it was a very treatable ailment and not the end of her road to reproductive success.

Back at home in the real world, it did not taste like good news. At this point a caring, sensitive specialist prepared to listen to her concerns and thoroughly investigate her problems was the order of the day. Instead, we got Dr Panties.

Dr Panties was a local gynaecologist who we quickly christened for his propensity to use the P-word when referring to women's underwear. Liz came back from each visit virtually untouchable, skin still crawling from the experience and the indefinable indignity the word, and therefore the man, represented to her. She hated him and I hated him just because she did. I never met him, but my overactive imagination painted a grim picture of their appointments together.

'Kindly remove your panties, Elizabeth.'

'Would you get on the table and take off your panties, please, Elizabeth.'

'Elizabeth, up on the table and panties off. Slowly now.'

'Are they some sweet new panties Elizabeeeeeth?' Okay, maybe that's going a bit far, but we've all seen *Silence of the Lambs*. In my eyes the consistent use of the P-word conjures images of a single man living alone in a house with a cellar, in which he capers around performing certain... acts... in front of a large mirror.

Is this unfair? Almost definitely. In her usual sympathetic style, Liz chose to try to put this minor annoyance to the back of her mind and look for the best in her new doctor, but she's a far better man than I. At best, with his experience in his line of work, I thought he was showing both a lack of empathy for the feelings of his patients and complete disregard of social mores. At worst, well, it's a small step from panty-caller to panty-sniffer.

On the first of many unpleasant visits, Dr Panties prescribed a drug called Clomid to help regulate Liz's periods and stimulate her ovaries to produce eggs at a predictable time in her cycle. Clomid works by tricking the brain into producing more oestrogen and thereby, hopefully, more eggs.

Our bedroom was quickly transformed from a bawdy love nest into the Lilyfield branch of the CSIRO.

Along with the magic pills that were to instantly fix all our problems came grid paper, a thermometer and an instructional leaflet. The idea was that Liz would pop a Clomid pill on days two to five of her cycle, and monitor her basal body temperature (her body's temperature completely at rest) before she got out of bed, which she would then chart on the grid paper. Around day twelve, the lowest dip in the graph would indicate ovulation and—whammo!—we'd get to work between the sheets and she'd have a bun in the oven before you could say, 'Good on you, Mum, Tip Top's the one.'

We soon discovered that in the real world—that is, the world outside the instructions included free with the ovulation thermometer—things aren't that easy.

During Liz's first cycle on Clomid we found that everything after the popping of the pill was harder than reading directions translated from Japanese. First off, the instruction sheet recommended that Liz take her temperature vaginally. There was no way she was going to put herself through a daily wake-up call that involved scrabbling around under the doona attempting to insert tab A into slot B. Apparently an alternative method was to simply stick the thermometer under your tongue, if you kept your mouth closed. Much easier.

The sample temperature chart that came with the thermometer predicted Liz's temperature would loiter around 36.6 degrees until day twelve of her cycle, when it would dive down to 36.3 and then rise all the way up to around 36.9 over a couple of days—a big jump when the whole chart covered only one degree Celsius. This ovulation zone was supposed to look like a big square-root sign on paper, after which her temperature would stay high until her next period. The two days either side of the big temperature drop are the most fertile and are the optimum time to be gettin' jiggy with it.

Liz dutifully started popping the pills and doing all the right things, but her temperature wasn't moving. In the first month we produced a graph that, despite all manner of dodgy interpretations, looked like a map of the Hume Highway—some slight turns but no real landmarks to get excited about. At least Liz wasn't experiencing the mood swings commonly associated with Clomid. Her moods swung wildly all right, but unless she was grinding up those little white pills and adding them to my tea, I was cooking up the very same symptoms all on my own.

After the first month we returned our thermometer twice claiming it was defective and got replacements that produced the same results. We had sex every couple of days around the middle of the cycle, but the lack of a definitive signpost made it feel like a stab in the dark in more ways than one.

It's funny. Liz and I have always enjoyed our luuurve-making—not in a shag-you-on-the-way-to-the-bus-stop kind of frenzied way, but we're just exceedingly compatible in the bedroom. I'd always thought that sex on demand would be kind of fun—'Get over here and *produce*, big boy'—but sex by the chart did take the shine off proceedings somewhat, and certainly robbed the act of a little spontaneity. But, to paraphrase the old pizza-is-like-sex simile, even chart sex was still pretty good, and to whine about this after what Liz had already been through would have been the height of churlishness.

Our chart-plotting exploits improved when I paid $29 for a digital ovulation thermometer. I realise now—now that the knowledge is frustratingly useless—that we weren't shaking the old-fashioned thermometers to get the mercury back down after we'd used them, so the reading never changed. I'd watched enough episodes of *ER* to know this manoeuvre and am still kicking myself over this blunder. But with a digital display correct to two decimal places, there were no such problems—aside from the beeping it made when it took a reading.

As a teacher with a long commute, Liz was always up early and therefore took her readings even earlier. I, on the other hand, enjoy my sleep and seem to require quite a lot of it. I blame a fast metabolism—hey, it sounds better than bone laziness. Whatever the case, I have no use for the number six on my bedside clock in the morning, so I came to dread the piercing beep which that lump of plastic spat out after it had taken its reading. One beep to start the test, three beeps when it finished. Grunt and roll over for another hour of shut-eye.

You may call me Sir Churlish Whineworthy of Ingrate Manor.

At the other end of the house, work was also progressing slowly.

The bamboo had been dug and poisoned repeatedly and had finally stopped sprouting, so construction on The Great Wall could begin. The first stage involved carefully undermining the bank of earth under the Besser block wall to add concrete footings under the wall to stabilise it. Looking up at the Great Wall from knee-deep in the trench below it, I swore it had tilted over me a degree or two and was threatening to collapse onto our house and my head. But I measured it and it seemed okay, so I tried to put this out of my mind and beavered on, digging, undermining, jackhammering, running for cover.

I don't think it was any accident that Liz sightings in the backyard were scarce during this period.

In January 2003, after my lightning morning raid on the pathology lab, my day of spermal reckoning finally arrived, despite all efforts to the contrary. After trying to joke, reason, argue and finally ignore my way past the issue, in the end I knew I had no option.

After I digested the GP's bad news, tossed off off-handedly like the sperm sample he was critiquing, life seemed to get slippery, like a flight of cartoon stairs that suddenly folds flat into a slide.

I couldn't quite grab a handhold each day. At work, I'd find myself drifting around or standing at the photocopier with a sheaf of papers in hand, staring at the wall and wondering what the point of this was, this copying, this job. If I couldn't get my wife pregnant and have kids, my priorities had to change, but to what? Put simply, what else was there?

I immediately blamed myself for our lack of conception, especially now Liz had her magic pill, prescribed by a bona fide (if slightly creepy) specialist doctor. If she was now fixed and we still had no result, there were no prizes for guessing where the finger of blame was now pointing.

In turn, I blamed a stint in the Royal Australian Air Force. I'd joined straight out of high school and graduated to work on fighter jet radar systems. During my time in one radar workshop, there was some anecdotal evidence to suggest that many more girls than boys were being born to men who worked there. *Clearly this meant that we were all being irradiated, that the small electromagnetic detectors we were issued with were mere paperweights and the Y chromosomes in our sperm were being massacred by the millions!*

This is not fucking fair!

THESEFUCKERSHAVESTOLENMYMANHOOD!

There were drunk women having sex with drug addicts in alleys and getting pregnant (I didn't know any personally but I'd seen them on TV) so why the hell can't we manage it? Why does this have to happen to *us*?

- If you smoke, don't, and also avoid smoky venues such as pubs. (I figured hanging around in pubs when you can't drink was masochistic to the point of lunacy anyway.)
- Drink buckets of purified water.
- Get plenty of sleep.
- Eat only organic meat and produce.
- Limit fruit to two or three pieces a day.
- Eat whole grains only.
- Give up soft drinks.
- Give up processed sugar.
- Give up chocolate.
- Get plenty of exercise, but keep your groin cool (that qualifier was directed more at me). Therefore you'll have to...
- Burn your Y-fronts (not during use).

After hearing all this and quickly calculating that, as of now, your entire diet will consist of organic carrot juice shakes and steamed potatoes, you are then told to avoid all forms of stress. Yes. That's right. Don't get (*remember to breathe*) worked up.

Happily, I have come up with a stress-reducing method of informing medicos how this kind of advice actually impacts on people in the real world. This is how it will work: we will simply get patients who have just simultaneously given up alcohol, smoking, coffee, sugar and chocolate—to gather and confront them. In their bedrooms. Late at night. Ah, think of it...our mild-mannered doctor wakes up in the wee small hours to find a dozen patients silently standing over him (or her) in the dark, and before he knows it this rabble of strung-out citizens are merrily reducing their stress by wringing his neck between swigs of their carrot juice frappés.

In the lead-up to my first sperm test, I had given up coffee (*sob*), wine (*sniff*), beer (*choke*), chocolate and soft drink (no hardship there). My added motivation to begin with was that these diet changes would theoretically improve my overall tadpole score. What a cruel joke that turned out to be. If that was the *new improved* count, I don't want to imagine what my groinular health was prior to my cleaning up my act.

For the next two years, I would stroll past coffee stands on my way to work sucking up lungfuls of those fine espresso fumes before arriving at my desk and treating myself to a weak cup of tea. I allowed myself two cups a day and drank filtered water until I felt like throwing up. I told friends and colleagues that I was on a health kick, that I had stopped abusing the body in which I lived. This was a version of the truth, but I was nowhere near ready to share with the world the reason for my detoxing.

Liz was even more strict. She had limited herself to one-teabag-dunk brews and had immediately given up wine, beer and, her supreme sacrifice, cake. Consequently, a wild Saturday night out for us involved a soup entree, a vegetarian main and a sugar-free cordial nightcap. If we were really letting our hair down we'd order lemon, lime and bitters, and then lie awake at night trying to calculate what evils were contained in three drops of alcohol.

Somewhere along the way we also learned that Liz had a wheat intolerance, which slimmed down her options even more, but improved her wellbeing out of sight once she adjusted her diet. Bread, pasta, cake and pastry were quickly struck from her already short dietary list, which meant she could eat pretty much anything, as long as it was rice, vegetables or tasted like packing foam.

We were both already pretty healthy on the exercise front. I managed to go to the gym three times a week without fail, with the odd run and swim thrown in for good measure, and Liz got her blood pumping by walking the dogs and taking on a nearby 7-kilometre bayside walking track a couple of times a week.

On those long evening walks with her friend Meeka, Liz and I would encounter the fruits of the inner west's countless recent labours. The region was in the middle of a reproductive purple patch. They were everywhere— babies of all shapes, sizes and shades parading past in titanium jogging prams, pushed by handsome couples laughing at the world, hair flowing in the breeze as their designer exercise clothing drew unsightly perspiration away from their perfect skin. You couldn't pause on a street corner without being mown down by battalions of strollers or gaggles of grinning mums and dads with the fruits of their loins hanging on their chests like medallions.

Friends, relatives, workmates ... everywhere we looked there seemed to be big bellies and vast 4WDs bursting at the seams with fecundity. Our next-door neighbours (her late thirties, him 40-plus) had a new little girl with blonde hair in bows; a friend around the corner (both he and his wife the wrong side of 40) had just taken delivery of their second. Where would it end? The flight path above the area was clearly not interfering with the stork's work, so when could we pencil ourselves into his schedule? Where was our unexpected surprise, our happy accident?

We tried not to let our anxiety build. We took foot baths, calming walks and pottered in the garden. We discussed the obvious merits of self-flagellation. Since low sperm counts and the inability to get your wife pregnant are not high on the list of water cooler discussion topics, I suffered in silence. I had good mates who would have heard me out, had I wanted to share my troubles, but how does a bloke react to a conversation-opener like that? 'Don't worry, mate. Erm... Hitler, he only had one ball.'

No, it would have been just too weird for all concerned.

Our working lives were also not without angst. After three years, Liz's application for a transfer to a school in the inner west had finally come good and, at the beginning of 2003, she started teaching at North Newtown Primary School. Of course, things at her new school were done differently and she felt like she had to prove herself all over again to her new peers. Her stress levels rose accordingly.

I, on the other hand, was bored at work, with no real prospects of advancement and spent my days dreaming of writing the great Australian novel. I could do the job on my ear, or on a wide range of other appendages, and felt like I was going precisely nowhere fast. For many people a comfortable, stable job is a godsend, but a job with no path to advancement can also look like a jail cell. For me, to be swimming towards something is infinitely more calming than treading water.

With this baggage on board, in mid-2003 we took a time-out between bouts of nitpicking and took stock of our goals, our lifestyle and the stress in our lives.

Our first priority was to stay married, a proposition on which the odds hadn't improved over the previous six months.

I can't recall the exact moment the word 'counselling' was uttered in our house but I believe it was around this time. Ten months into our marriage and the verbal fisticuffs were as fierce as ever. The good times were becoming mere brief respites between bad times and we hadn't a clue what to do about it. Both of us silently wondered if this was what marriage was really about, and if so, could we stand it? Maybe all this chasing of a baby was a folly. Maybe we were better off pulling the pin on the relationship before there was a child involved that could be royally screwed up by a pair of combative, separated parents. I'd experienced two divorces as a child and tapping for attention on the inside of my skull was the night when I was woken up and dragged bleary-eyed to the front door to be confronted with a man I had never met—a man my stepfather told me I had to go and live with because he was my new dad.

I would not be putting a child through that experience.

One night when things looked their blackest, we turned the TV off and sat looking at each other. The silence stretched. Every time we did this I was surer I'd be sleeping alone that night.

More silence.

Jesus, it really is the 'I'm leaving' speech this time...

Liz swallowed and finally lifted her gaze from the floor. 'So what are we doing here?'

And from that low point, slowly, steadily, we began tunnelling down to the burning kernels of anger, disappointment and frustration that were stuck in our relationship's craw. Over many months we attacked it, turned it upside down and shook the loose change from it. What we discovered was a fundamental misunderstanding that had been going on for some time.

Allow me to provide a classic example, and one that many a male unfortunate will relate to.

Liz: 'God I feel gross. I need a hair colour and I tried on those new pants I bought the other week and they're feeling a bit snug.'

Jason, spying a readily defined problem: 'Why don't you go for a run? Give Meeka a call. She'll go with you.'

Liz (annoyed now): 'This is the point at which you're supposed to say how beautiful I am and make me feel better and be on my side.'

Jason (angry): 'Of course I think you're beautiful; I'm just trying to help.'

Liz: 'So your version of helping is pointing out I should be doing more exercising? Are you dense? You know you never say nice things about me.'

Jason (turning on the TV): 'If you'll cast you mind back 30 seconds, I just said I thought you were beautiful.'

Liz: '*It doesn't count when I have to ask!*'

This is a very straightforward example but the underlying chalk-and-cheese support issues bubbled to the surface in a thousand ways, in myriad different situations. The end result, however, was always the same. Liz would feel like I wasn't on her side, she wasn't supported and I thought she was incapable of solving her own problems. I would feel unloved because she didn't want my help, and didn't appreciate that all I wanted to do was solve her problems, protect her and make her happy. Fixing stuff and solving problems makes me happy, so surely she would go about it the same way, right?

Wrong. Wrong approach, wrong attitude, wrong sex, fella. That *Men Are From Mars, Women Are From Venus* guy was onto something.

With a few D&Ms under our belts, after really, really baring our souls and laying it all on the line, we began to unearth this concept and understand the problem-solver versus nurturer issue we had.

Soon I began to practise empathising rather than solving. Initially, this behavioural retraining all seemed a bit false, like I was struggling against a few millions years of chest-beating caveman evolution. But any reservations I had gradually dissipated in line with the improvement in our relationship. Basically, if it meant a reduction in our constant sniping and fighting, it was a small price to pay.

After our little revelation, Liz also began to readjust her approach. When I reverted to my problem-solving ways, she would resist the urge to berate me, and instead gently remind me that she just needed a sympathetic ear. I'd apologise and supply two. Liz would bitch and moan and get things off her chest, I would listen and agree that, yes, the freaky woman at the bank *was* a cow and had probably been dropped as a child.

Suddenly it was us against the world again.

With the relationship on the improve we could refocus our attention on getting pregnant, but we found ourselves trapped by a common irony. In jockeying for a decent position from which to have the baby—house in the suburbs (with accompanying mortgage monster) and jobs in the city—we were becoming more stressed and putting more pressure on the marriage, without which we wouldn't commit to having a baby.

Somehow someone had flipped a switch and the Sydney we knew and loved seemed bent on doing our heads in. Everywhere we looked the traffic seemed worse, the pollution thicker, the population denser, the daylight hours shorter. We enjoyed our little cottage, and loved the area we lived in, but no matter how many renovation projects we completed the walls kept closing in.

Somewhere along the way, our random rumblings and mumblings of a seachange started to be given serious consideration. What was really stopping us? We'd miss our friends, but many of them had moved away or overseas. My mum lived in South Australia and I'd lost contact with my stepdad, so my only family ties in Sydney were with Liz's family. Liz's mum and dad—that would be our big loss. But, we figured they'd visit, there was always the telephone, and you never knew, they might follow us if there was a baby in the picture. We reckoned we would see Liz's brother and sister-in-law only slightly less often in the country or interstate than we did on the other side of Sydney.

'Think about it,' Liz said. 'Lower mortgage, a bigger house, maybe you could work part-time and write that book you're always messing with, and we could just, y'know ... slow down. If I got pregnant, we might actually have time to enjoy the baby.'

I rubbed my chin and tried not to look too excited. 'You know, it's just crazy enough to work.'

As we continued to mull over the ins and outs of transforming ourselves into jobless, homeless street people, I began to obsess over real estate websites, as is my wont.

'Whoa, you can get a fair bit for your money in Tassie.'

'Who do we know in Tasmania?'

'What about Perth? You went there once...'

'Yes, and it's great, but same problem. We could always go and live with your mum in South Australia.'

'I'll keep looking, shall I?'

Eventually a plan crystallised. What if we sold our house in Sydney, packed in our jobs and moved to Brisbane? Liz's grandparents and aunt had lived in the northern suburbs of Brisbane for years and Liz and her brother had been spending school holidays in the Sandgate area their whole lives. Tucked away on the northern shore of Moreton Bay, it still exudes the relaxed holiday feel and village atmosphere of a suburb built around a nineteenth-century town hall and post office, with lagoons, bay beaches and beautiful Queenslanders all around. Liz had always raved about the place and had once taken me up there visiting. It made a good first impression, so I said okay. I am not a hard sell.

So, before we had time to consult the tarot or read the leftover chicken giblets, the decision was made. We looked at each other in wonder as the adrenaline of a major life decision began to kick in. Now we knew how Kermit and Fozzie felt in *The Muppet Movie* when they almost collided with that fork in the road.

A few months later, after almost seven months of weekend toil, with the benefit of few power tools and even fewer assistants, The Great Wall of Lilyfield had been completed to wild celebrations (in my head) and universal acclaim (among our dogs). We celebrated with backyard drinks, and our friends turned up and kindly oo-ed and ahhh-ed in all the right places. In the central third of the raised bed at the foot of the wall, an underwater light illuminated a small pond complete with bubbling fountain, lilies and rushes with six tiny but very tame carp swimming amongst them. In the raised beds either side of the water feature, small lilli pillies flanking mandarin trees, and star jasmine crept up mesh fixed to the sandstone-rendered wall. Spotlights were trained on the wall and on a large mosaic of a heron that Liz and

I made for above the pond. It all looked a picture, even if I do say so me-self.

In the bedroom, our issues were proving more difficult to crack.

After six months on Clomid, Liz's cycle was only marginally more predictable, our graphs were all over the place and our prayers remained unanswered. What both of us had seen as our easy-fix wonder drug actually seemed to be having very little effect on anything but our bank balance. We also saw a naturopath who had suggested a litany of supplements to help my troops fight the good fight but, aside from tasting like the stuff road crews fill potholes with, they brought no miracles either.

As each fruitless month passed, we doubted our bodies and ourselves a little more. There was just no way to tell what was or wasn't going on down there. Why couldn't we introduce the sperm to the eggs out in the open, say, over lunch at the races when both have a few champagnes under their belts? Anything but these million-to-one covert operations under cover of darkness, with no reports, no feedback and no control.

Was my ragtag battalion of swimmers just not up to the long journey to the land of ovum, or were there just not enough of them to mount a charge? Was Liz even producing eggs at roughly the right time for them to rendezvous with? There was still a slight chance that our timing had been minutely off and everything was set to work if only our genetic material would meet on a romantic stroll in the fallopian tube. As it was, we were still fumbling around in the dark with our fumbling around in the dark.

Using the chart method to pick the most fertile period seemed to rely on an oddly retrospective count-back system. *Your temperature dipped? Fantastic! Two of your most fertile days have just passed. Better get horizontal quick smart or you can shut up shop for another month.*

This is fine if you are blessed with a cycle by Seiko, but our graphs weren't doing what they were supposed to do, so we were relying on pure guesswork. In the end we just had sex every two days through the middle of Liz's cycle. Needless to say, when your foreplay consists of silent counting on your fingers and a 'Come on then, let's get at it', one's sex life is robbed of a small slice of joy.

So there we were, searching for our graph's square root and rooting every other day anyway, marking each coupling with a romantic little x on our chart. Our research threw up differing opinions on how long the sperm (2–5 days?) and eggs (12–24 hours?) can last in the reproductive tract, and upon the monthly fourteen-day post-period count-back, using minimum specs, we never seemed to have quite got the timing right.

Were we a couple of hours late? Does the twelve-hour countdown start with the egg at the top or bottom of the fallopian tube?

Maybe the sperm have to be loitering *in* the tube when the egg descends.

How long do they take to swim up that far?

Should Liz stand on her head to help out?

Madness was not far away.

The months passed and we started to despair. It began to look like test tubes would soon become involved. I know it's wrong, but oh, how we envied all those teenagers getting knocked up after one sandy indiscretion at schoolies week.

After a river of blood, sweat and curse words, the renovation was complete and it was time to auction our lovely Lilyfield cottage. A fortnight before the big day, there were eight contracts in circulation and things were looking rosy. Then aliens began abducting our buyers.

A series of frantic phone calls throughout the last week cast a pall over our auction prospects.

Even our agent's comical Irish accent couldn't sugar-coat the news. 'Guys, I dinno why but all ur buyers seem to have gon inta hidin''

'I thought we had five solid bidders?'

'Dat's what I tought too, but one lot bought sumptin' else, and I can't get a holda two more. I tink we've only got two solid prospects left. But you nevva know on de day.'

Joy. Our auction-day dreams of a carnival atmosphere with vast crowds of bidders shouting themselves hoarse, great wads of cash spilling from every pocket, faded to scenes of an auctioneer roaring away to an empty street while a tiny cricket chirped in the background.

Auction day began with one of those crisp November mornings full of fragrance, dewy blossoms and the promise of warmer things to come. We embarked on our usual cleaning frenzy, and when we next looked up it was time to hit 'repeat' on the chill-out CD, get the dogs ready and hoof it to the nearest park while people we'd never met tramped dirt through our house.

The news from our Irishman had not improved. Buyers who had dropped out remained uninterested despite calls that must have verged on harassment and he hadn't managed to scare up new ones to replace them. He was confident that he had one in the bag, with the other one a 50/50 chance. But we weren't to worry. Anything could happen on the day.

Luckily I was way past worry and had boarded a speeding train midway from Panic Station to Complete Terror Junction. As per usual, the build-up of adrenaline in my veins quickly led to a build-up of pressure in my bowels, and ten minutes into our enforced hour of absence I made a beeline for the squat brick toilet block that occupies a corner of Rozelle's Easton Park. I handed the dogs to Liz and did the Cliff Young shuffle to the building, clenching for all I was worth.

Locked! Men's *and* women's! I robot-walked back to Liz and the dogs, and sat down hard on the park bench, stood up and sat down hard again. We were casting about for something to dig a hole with when the Irishman pulled up nearby looking flustered.

'Howarye, guys? Just a couple o queries. One o the bidders wants te know if you'll mind a coupla changes to da contract.'

I suspect wholesale changes to contracts on auction day are always a hard sell, but this Irishman's eyes had ceased smiling and he looked determined to go toe-to-

toe on this one. He'd worked fookin' hard for his sale and he wanted his commission sewn up that day. Then he took one look at my face, suddenly agreed to our terms and drove away. I was puzzled by his sudden change of heart, but there was an auction to go to, so I wiped the tears from my bulging eyes, loosened my belt even further and we started the long, painful walk home.

On the way, Liz and I discussed the possibility of living a very modest lifestyle in Brisbane. Possibly under an overpass somewhere. Clearly an auction with one bidder is never going to be a raging success, and it was likely we'd have to drop our expectations. Once the bank was paid off, the kitty for any new house might be a little mangier than we'd planned.

By the time we entered the small crowd that had gathered outside our house, we agreed that we would live in a caravan without (*gasp*) a TV if it meant that we'd be together with the dogs and without the time-poor lifestyle and high mortgage. That made me feel better. After I sprinted to the toilet, I felt better still.

As I sat there with the bomb bay doors open, I wondered what I'd find when I emerged. Would the auctioneer be shouting into silence like I'd imagined? If there was only one bidder and they were smart, they'd bid once, let the place be passed in and then put in a low post-auction offer. Or would there be no bids at all? Could they call it off altogether?

I flung open the door and strode off through a cloud of air freshener to the front bedroom to listen with Liz to the auctioneer's opening spiel.

The ruddy-faced bloke was already in full swing and over the reserve! The *optimistic* reserve!

I crept up next to Liz and joined her kneeling on the bed, peering out the window, lungs frozen and mouths agape. There were two bidders after all, and by the pace of the action, they both really wanted our humble cottage.

The figure went up another $10,000. We collapsed on the bed, biting our hands.

Then another $10,000.

Then the well ran dry. The bidding had stalled and the Irishman gravely stepped inside to 'confer' with his vendors, both of whom were lying on their backs on their bed, silently doing the cockroach with glee. That would be a yes, my good man; knock it down.

Phase one of the baby master plan was complete.

THE WORLD
ACCORDING TO
CARP

Like many successful renovators, when considering a second project Liz and I were confident that we would rather live in a refrigerator box on the side of a highway than do it all again. So in searching for our new home in Brisbane our only criteria were that it was fully renovated and had a deck on which we could sip mixed drinks, scratch ourselves and remark on the weather. That's what Queenslanders did with their days, right?

With such stringent criteria and with a home that was a whole 4.3 metres wide to live up to, maybe it wasn't surprising that it took us precisely six hours of house-hunting to find our new address.

Allow me to explain.

A week after the auction hammer had fallen on our Lilyfield cottage, we booked a weekend trip to Brisbane, our pockets bulging with the theoretical dollars from our buyers. I teed up a packed Saturday schedule of inspections, and we pounded the pavements of Sandgate searching for our dream home.

The day passed in a blur of large-toothed estate agents, 70s paisley carpeting and backyards oozing an odourless, colourless gas called 'potential'. After specifying that we were looking for a renovated Queenslander, we saw high-set palm-fringed haciendas, low-set brick bungalows and fixer-uppers with only the loosest claim on the term 'Queenslander' (they were in the right state). Eight houses into a ten-house schedule, our excitement quickly being replaced by fatigue, Liz, her nan and I came upon The One.

It was a high-set 50s-style weatherboard Queenslander with a tiled roof and a vast deck that dominated the entire rear of the house. The landscape gardener owner had surrounded the house with tropical gardens and added a waterfall water feature in one corner of the backyard and a boardwalk along one side of the house. Inside was spacious with three bedrooms opening off the living room and a large kitchen beside a dining room with two sets of French doors opening onto the deck.

As soon as Nan and I walked inside, we shared a quick 'yes, please' look, but carefully out of the agent's sight. Cunningly we also refrained from dancing a highland fling and screaming, 'We'll take it!' Instead, I rubbed my chin and looked thoughtful. You should see me play poker.

Liz also liked the house even though two of her main criteria—a new kitchen and bathroom—weren't fully met, and we quickly won her over. Soon we were in Sandgate village on the other side of the agent's desk, listening to one side of the phone negotiations with the owners, and we slapped down a deposit the next day.

Aside from the great weather and natural beauty of the area, the trip had been another chance to get a feel for the pace of Brisbane. Despite growing up on the far north coast of New South Wales, I didn't know Brisbane well, and by all accounts the city had undergone something of a transformation in the last decade anyway.

Brisbane struck me as a progressive city that has still retained some of its laid-back country-town friendliness, no mean feat for a capital with a population of 1.8 million. Walking around suburban streets, it was not uncommon for strangers to smile and offer a friendly hello. As Sydneysiders we found this a tad confronting and I hope none of the locals were too put out by our eyes-to-the-ground-shy-smile reactions. If they didn't notice us instinctively reaching for our Mace, I'd say it was a victory. A city where people still look each other in the eye? What kind of madcap topsy-turvy community had we bought into?

Back at home, in mid-November 2003 Sydney's streets were awash with rabid rugby fans and average Sydneysiders were actually displaying the kind of open good humour not seen since the year 2000, when the city kicked up its heels to welcome back thousands of its more stupid residents who had fled to the country to escape the terrifying 'millennium bug'. Living so close to the city and the Homebush sports complex, we encouraged our rugby-loving friends to come on down and our friends from Canberra, Sari and Mark, took advantage of our invitation and lobbed for a couple of days of intense beer lout-ery, with a game or two of international rugby thrown in.

We hadn't seen the couple we will forever refer to with the collective SariandMark, as if they shared a single brain, for months but we soon slipped back into our comfortable familiarity. We were having a great laugh over a few drinks in our backyard—I was enjoying a light beer and it was such a special occasion that Liz was even sipping a rare glass of wine—and suddenly I could tell something large was about to happen. Our friends had a secret and, in a grinning rush, coughed up the good news that they were pregnant.

I will preface this by saying that I was born with a congenital abnormality. Somehow I seem to have developed in the womb without the part of the brain that directs a human being's face to display one emotion while, mere centimetres away, their brain is experiencing another. I think in some circles they call it 'acting' (in others 'lying'). Suffice it to say that if I was forced into a stage play at gunpoint the quality of my performance would fall somewhere between the work of a drunk Dolph Lundgren and that of a length of two-by-four. Throughout my life this has caused untold angst, especially at birthdays and Christmases.

Gift-giver: 'Merry Christmas, Jase—it's that six-pack of Rainbow Brite underwear you've had your eye on.'

Me (looking like I was handed a leaking bag of ocelot parts): 'Yeah, thanks. Can I have the plastic compass from your cracker?'

It's not that I'm mean, or ungrateful, it's just that my face reacts before I can stop it. Thankfully my disability is short-lived and, if I quickly employ a series of cunning distractionary techniques I have learned in my years on Earth, I can continue to function within human society.

So, when Mark told us the happy news of his impending fatherhood, my mouth opened, my eyes widened and I knew to quickly bend down to slap a non-existent mosquito on my leg. On the way up I had time to subtly change my involuntary surprise-horror face into the more acceptable surprise-joy version and toast the parents to be. I should have been a secret agent.

The truth is I *was* happy for them but the happiness couldn't get its head above the high tide of devastation boiling in my brain. I have no idea why, but that particular pregnancy seemed to be the one that affected me most, even amid the massive landslide of fertility we'd seen around us. Who was going to be next to spring the surprise fatherhood announcement? Molly Meldrum? The Pope?

It took several more hissing sessions in the kitchen 'getting more nibblies' before Liz could get me to apply some sort of perspective to the situation. Yes, we knew they had probably been trying and, no, it doesn't mean there was one less left in the universal 'bucket of pregnancies'. Just be happy and don't spoil it for them, okay?

This proved difficult when our own reproductive landscape was starting to feel like a NASA space probe photo of the surface of Mars. With Liz organising a school musical and madly writing end-of-year reports in the evenings and me working longer hours and dealing with removalists, solicitors and suddenly unmotivated real estate professionals in my spare moments, our bedroom work during that period was certainly not the greatest of our collective career.

When we weren't too shagged to shag, we never had sex without considering the repercussions on my sperm first. We couldn't afford to. In trying to buck the astronomical odds we'd been quoted, there was no telling just what tiny parameters of volume and timing would tip the balance in our favour. Liz was still dutifully taking her Clomid and I my various supplements but was any of it working, or even helping, even a weensy bit?

It all started to take on a slightly sour, futile flavour. In sporting parlance, heads were starting to drop in Team Davis as the side already found itself struggling to penetrate some solid defence early in the first half.

Not to worry, though—our knight in shining lab coat, Dr Panties, had proven himself to be totally inept in all facets of fertility medicine, apart from the ability to incite hatred in his patients at twenty paces. Happily, Liz saw the writing on the wall (I assume it was a floor-to-ceiling sign that said 'Hey, chickybabes, please remove your

PANTIES') and got a referral to a specialist in Brisbane. That innocuous white envelope was the key to our first foray into the world's most bittersweet acronym: IVF.

Meanwhile, we had entered the alcohol-soaked Christmas party season, and I found it impossible to maintain my semi-abstinence during a fortnight in which my working week was studded with boozy lunches, leaving parties and Christmas shindigs. As well as the general end-of-year festivities, I was pulling the pin on my job and had made some good friends in my time there, so there was no shortage of colleagues on hand to help me reaffirm my acquaintance with the bottle.

Clearly this was the optimum time to have another sperm test.

My GP had mentioned something about a confirmation test as I stormed out of his office cursing innocent receptionists and lashing out at pot plants last time, and I wanted to go to Queensland with a full set of facts for whatever new (and hopefully competent) doctor we saw there. Liz tried to talk me out of it, but why not do one during the silly season? I'd looked after myself last time and the result had been—how can I put it?—shite, so maybe a long stint of abusing myself (before the short stint of abusing myself) would see things improve. I just didn't believe the whole clean-living kick had made a jot of difference and, more than that, I was well past giving a toss. So to speak.

So, another day, another yellow-lidded jar and another private session of waxing the dolphin. When I think that

that may have been the last thing I did on our furniture before the men came to take it away, I get a little teary.

But time and sweaty bands of removalists move on. Soon the last box had been loaded onto the truck and we were sweeping out the dust bunnies from the corners of our empty house and handing over our last set of keys. Our time was up and, after a few loving strokes of the woodwork while no-one was looking we turned our backs on the dodgy cottage we had miraculously transformed into a slightly less dodgy cottage. We were homeless and on the move.

There were two weeks of work to get through before our stint as jobless hoboes could begin, so I packed a bag and went to stay with my former flatmate and his girlfriend in a flat in beachside Coogee while Liz took the dogs and moved in with her brother and sister-in-law in the western suburbs. Our six affectionate carp were plucked from the water feature in the Great Wall and plonked into their new home, the most luxurious plastic travel tank with air pump that $15 can buy, and went with her.

From my perspective this arrangement was great—it was a chance to relive my carefree Coogee days with my old mate Andrew and have a few nights out on the town. Liz, on the other hand, was lumbered with the responsibility of looking after the dogs and making sure they settled in to their new environment and new backyard. Cunningly I played down the riotous fun I was having and emphasised the pining away angle.

The pub was a real morgue, dear. I think someone in the back bar was playing a harmonica.

On one of my last days of work I got a call from Liz, obviously panicked, to say that our kids had been found wandering the streets of Kellyville and had been dropped back into the yard by a kindly neighbour. Thank Christ we had the foresight to get their temporary phone number engraved on their dog tags and thank double-Christ for the great neighbours who returned them.

On the other side of town, with great trepidation, I dropped in to my GP's offices to pick up an innocuous sheet of white paper. On it was a set of figures that had the power to drag me back into the virile land of the average male or send me ashamed and alone into that eunuch-filled shadow-world populated by men of the calibre of Humphrey B. Bear and those two guys from Hi-5.

I tried to stop my hand shaking long enough to read the page. Scanning through the disclaimers ... explanatory notes ... ancillary figures—here it is—8 million/ml.

Wow, that sounds like a lo ... *JESUS H. CHRIST ON A POPSICLE STICK, THAT'S HALF AS MUCH AS LAST TIME!*

Luckily I was on a bus at the time, so I was already sitting down. The great thing about public transport is that when your head starts spinning and you find yourself feeling woozy there are plenty of things to hang onto: your seat, the handrails, the hair of the person in the seat in front of you.

This was by far the lowest point in my journey so far. The reading was so low as to be negligible and quickly squashed what little hope I held of one day becoming a father. No first steps, no first 'dada', no kisses on scraped knees or wobbly training sessions on shiny red first bicycles. My high-stress beer-swilling lifestyle had caught up with me, tapped me on the shoulder and delivered the killer blow. Needless to say, when I got back to the flat Andrew and I made a beeline for the pub.

For those who still believe in the tooth fairy and generous tax cuts, let me be the one to break the news that life is not always fair. Even though Liz had advised me not to do my follow-up sperm test during the annual end-of-year Stress and Beer festival, she was the one who wore the consequences. I was grumpy, I was sullen, I was grouchy. Instead of supporting her in the wash-up of her semi-traumatic dog escape episode, I just focused on myself and the black hole my second sperm test had drop-kicked me into.

After a week apart we arranged an early-morning rendezvous back at our old Rozelle stomping ground, but I was pretty poor company. Liz and the dogs were full of beans and keen to see me and I was keen to kick at the ground and snipe at anything and anyone within my field of vision.

This led to one of our more explosive arguments. Looking back, I struggle to comprehend how I could have built myself any moral high ground from which to wage a verbal war that day, but build it I did, using a matrix of twisted logic, circular arguments and pointed accusations. I don't remember how we eventually reconciled, but it's safe to assume it was all Liz's doing. I would nominate her for a Nobel Peace Prize, but Bono has stolen all the forms.

Without those pesky jobs to cramp our style, we fled to recharge our batteries in South Australia.

We spent our first ten days with my mum in Victor Harbor, on the beautiful Fleurieu Peninsula south of Adelaide. After sleeping away the first 48 hours, we settled in for long bouts of sitting on the deck, sunning ourselves and contemplating our navels. It was bliss: walking on the beach, short day trips and long glasses of red. We had kept my mum up to date with our procreative struggles without furnishing her with all the gory details and she had been diligently praying for us at her local church.

In the last half-dozen years my relationship with Mum had slowly healed. For years I had held a lingering resentment towards her for what I saw as some poor parenting choices she made during her second marriage break-up, but time must have mellowed me. I guess the more life throws at you, the more you see that decisions made in chaotic times are not so cut and dried and that the view from the inside of the maelstrom must be very different. Pointing fingers from the sidelines helps nobody, nor does harbouring resentment. I was gradually letting it go.

She had not had an easy life. After emigrating from the north of England when she was a sixteen-year-old in 1966, most of her family quickly returned but Mum persevered in her new country, carving out a life that had its share of ups and downs and years of hard graft. After two divorces and a string of long-term but failed relationships with men Mum had reverted back to her maiden name of Jennifer Lamb, and was finally happy in her own skin, just being single and running her own race. It showed. She was more relaxed, more contented and gaining a lot of satisfaction from throwing herself into her community work.

Mum had loved Liz from the get-go, and the three of us continued to bond during the trip. Our shoulders gradually unknotted, our breath deepened and I even got through the Christmas period without my usual dose of bah-humbuggery. Crosswords were done, mobile phones were prised from ears, and after a few days, I actually went 24 hours without turning mine on! If you can imagine.

We were having a great time, but Liz and my relationship also needed some attention, so we took off for a few days on Kangaroo Island, off the southern tip of South Australia. Stepping off the ferry onto this pristine animal playground is a bit like rewinding 30 years, to a less populated, less troubled Australia. We hoped the relaxed lifestyle and lack of twenty-first-century pollutants and pressures might lead to a spontaneous conception.

It was a refreshing change to hop into bed without counting days and consulting paperwork and we found some of the frivolity leaking back into our rumpy-pumpy. The bed in our room was soft and we left it a touch softer, but managed to fit in some swimming, penguin tours and seal-watching into our meagre sixteen hours of free time every day. A couple of days at a hotel in

Adelaide and New Year's Eve with my old friend Bart at the end of the holiday added to the fun and left us invigorated and ready for the next chapter in our pro-creational plan. There was even a slight blip of excitement as our trusty beeping thermometer informed us that Liz's temperature was high. If we counted back, hey... we might've finally got our timing right!

But we'd been through false dawns like that before. Now was not the time to be sitting around daydreaming, it was time to pack the car to the roof, hightail it over the border and never look back.

Hindsight is a truly wondrous thing. After our experience in early January 2004 driving interstate with a car full of animals, now when sitting down to carefully plan a road trip I always recommend taking along at least half a dozen carp.

When carrying your fishy passengers, you'll need to keep them in a small travel tank, but you'll also have to guard against water spillage. Try placing the tank inside an Esky with the lid propped open to allow airflow. That way you'll be able to drive the best part of 1000 km with a sloshing sound coming from the back seat while constantly waiting to be hit in the back of the head by a wave of flying fishwater. But don't worry, the danger is at its greatest only when performing sudden and dangerous car manoeuvres like driving over slight bumps or turning.

Liz and I investigated many different options for getting our pets to Queensland by air, but none sounded

safe enough, so we bought little seatbelt harnesses for
Bob and Matilda, belted in the Esky full of carp securely
on the back seat, threw in clothes and camping gear and
hit the highway.

We were jobless itinerants, so we had as much time
as we needed to wend our way up the coast to Brisbane
and it was just as well. The excitement of the journey
had Bob and Tilly lapping regularly at their water bowl
so they needed a piddle stop about every 90 minutes.
Then after each fifteen-minute wee break in the January
sun, they'd be dehydrated and take on a bellyful of water
to do it all again.

But progress was made, Coffs Harbour came and went
and with the sun dipping into the west I pushed on and
found a caravan park near the beach in sleepy Woolgoolga.

On the rare occasions I enter a van park, I always
swear I can hear the sound of tobacco being chawed
and banjos being plucked. Remember, this is their
community—a community where law enforcement consists
of an overweight manager called Nev with a torch and
a walking stick, tapping on tents and growling, 'That
better be a herbal cigarette.'

We were allocated a luxurious four-by-four-metre
patch of grass between a row of permanent vans and a
tranquil creek. Trying to wrangle two excited hounds
while pegging out a tent with one hand and arranging
bedding with the other foot made me long for a cold
one, but foolishly I had forgotten to buy any beers. Then,
minutes later, the gods looked like they'd provided.

Apparently the amiable family in the 42-foot, three-bedroom tent beside us didn't feel like roughing it by making do with their 50-litre electric fridge and barbecue combo, so Uncle Barry had turned up with a flatbed truck carrying—I kid you not—a full-sized Kelvinator. But there he was, scratching his head, looking at his small and distinctly female relatives and wondering how he was going to get the white monolith off the truck.

So I stepped up, did the neighbourly thing and offered to help him lift it down.

We grabbed the fridge's razor-like bottom rails and wrestled it to the ground listening to our kneecaps crack and pop like the morning's Rice Bubbles. As soon as we took the weight and I felt my discs bulge I figured the bloke had filled it before moving it, but shut my trap and concentrated on the beers within. We got the fridge down and dragged it up to their tent door, next to the karaoke machine and party strobe light. Some of the sweat from my brow had run into the corners of my mouth and perhaps I was less than subtle in licking my lips and wiping my mouth, but Uncle Barry seemed to get the message. Like an angel of mercy the big, lovable lunk stopped rearranging his innumerable cold stubbies, turned to me, stuck out his hand and offered it to me to shake.

Van park folk are friendly like that.

The next morning we were up before the birds and packed up the campsite in record time. Our animals looked fresh and happy, but their chauffeurs were both shattered after a restless night of driving their hips into the rocky ground through a patchwork of blankets and towels. Still, we were a mere five hours from our new home and ready to start our new life.

Somewhere near the border Matilda started to look decidedly ill and was making odd noises with her head slumped over the edge of the back seat. We averted disaster through frequent rest stops, but another half-hour on the road and she was again somehow looking green through her dark Hairy Maclary mop.

The tension was palpable. She was a panting time bomb. Would we get to the house before she sicked all over the back seat, possibly setting off a chain reaction that would lead all the way down to the six carp spitting up tiny chucks of fish flakes over each other? Or would we avert disaster by getting her into the house and curled up under a bed in time? In the major motion picture adaptation of the situation, I will be played by Matt Damon, Liz will be played by Catherine Zeta-Jones and, in a shock casting decision, Matilda will be played by Linda Blair.

Just when we were seriously considering stopping to buy a bucket we were off the freeway and three streets from home. Result! The great interstate zoological road trip was over, with the carp still alive and sloshing side-to-side like half-pipe snowboarders, Bob still asleep as usual, Liz and I still alert and sane, and Matilda vomiting a puddle of last night's fish and chips all over the back seat upholstery.

Seconds later we pulled up outside our new house.

Welcome to Queensland.

ACRONYM WARS

The next time you're watching a movie in which the hero wakes up one morning to find the streets of his village/town/city completely deserted, do not immediately assume (like I do) that a doomsday virus has turned the inhabitants into homicidal hatchet-wielding zombies. It's far more likely the entire population of Bumfluff, North Dakota, is at the local IVF clinic fighting over a number for their 7am blood test.

After a couple of weeks of settling in to our new home, Liz and I bit the bullet and made an appointment to see a doctor at the Queensland Fertility Group (QFG), the epicentre of IVF treatment in Brisbane.

Clutching our referral from Dr Panties, we turned up at the city's medical precinct in leafy Spring Hill. It felt like we were striking out on our own, medical pioneers in a new city about to kick in some doors and demand answers to all our reproductive quandaries. Gee, I couldn't wait to hang around a deserted waiting room, periodically pinging the reception bell and announcing loudly that we needed to see someone about 'our downstairs problems'.

We had our work cut out getting noticed all right— it was the most frantic medical centre I have ever seen.

If we'd done any kind of research, we would have known that assisted fertility is big business in Australia, with almost 3 per cent of all babies born now conceived using IVF or another kind of assisted reproduction. That's a hell of a lot of couples succeeding, and many more trying to get help, and they all seemed to have appoint-ments at QFG. We'd step out of the QFG elevator at 7.10am expecting a morgue, only to find the nurses' station under siege with couples picking up numbers, filling out paperwork and milling around wondering how everyone got there before them. Every time we went there the waiting room was jumping, every seat filled by young professional couples, long-suffering 40-somethings and mothers with tots already on their knees (what, must they hog *all* the babies?). The children would be cooed at and occasionally a noticeably pregnant woman would walk in, to the slightly jealous looks of all present. We sat quietly among the milieu watching couples disappearing into the doctor's room and tried to gauge their expressions when they reappeared. Then it was our turn.

Our doctor was a forthright kind of guy who, as he admitted, was all about the end result. We'll call him

Doctor Smith, for his sense of humour was about as warm and contagious as that of the po-faced Doctor Smith of *Lost In Space* fame. Non-funnily enough, his impassive assistant reminded me of The Robot, although I never actually saw her wave her arms around and yell 'Danger! Danger!' Perhaps that circuit kicks in in the event of a fire.

What I liked most about Dr Smith was his confidence. Our fertility specialist quickly informed us that he had one of the best pregnancy rates in the country, and his bulldozer attitude seemed capable of sweeping aside even the most major of fertility crises. Got PCOS? He knew it backwards, forwards and sideways in the pike position. Low sperm count? He'd gotten couples pregnant using a single sperm with a limp. Don't give it a second thought.

He quickly went through our individual problems, the treatment we'd received thus far and the options for getting us pregnant. After shaking his head at the slipshod Clomid methodology used by good old Dr Panties, he assured us that Liz's relative youth made a pregnancy more likely and if the rest of her plumbing was in good shape, he was confident her PCOS could be overcome. As for me, presented with dismal sperm figures of 15 million/ml and 8 million/ml, I expected the doc to shake his head and pull out his dustiest medical tome in search of medical precedents. To my astonishment, he was very upbeat. Although the 8 million/ml reading wasn't anything to write home about, he said the first figure was only marginally outside normal limits, and was 'plenty of sperm to play with'. I was so excited that

the distasteful imagery didn't even sink in. He said it
was possible I'd just had an off day when I submitted
the second sample, fairly likely given the drinking I was
doing at the time, or maybe I'd just had a spectacular
result the first time. I was cheering for option number
one. The doctor said we could do another test to get a
better idea of my usual range, but that he'd gotten couples
pregnant with far lower readings, so it didn't really matter
either way.

Unfortunately Smith's focus on the end result seemed
to also include getting through as many patients as
humanly possible in the shortest amount of time. He had
the warm, caring bedside manner of a floor lamp and
we quickly realised that calm, considered, reassuring
discussion was not his thing. He fired the facts at you
like a Melbourne Cup race caller, with special emphasis
on percentage pregnancy rates, and it was up to you to
digest them licketty-split. If there was a decision to be
made, spit it out and say goodbye. He made our heads
spin, but he was pleasant in a mechanical kind of way
and his confidence was a breath of fresh air.

Given our ages and reproductive and general health,
Doctor Smith quoted us overall odds of getting pregnant
of more than 70 per cent through the life of our treatment.
That was 70, not 17. I sat in a chair on the other side
of his desk trying to process this, after every health care
professional we had seen thus far had looked at our
results, pulled a face and virtually shooed us out the door.

This guy's saying it might take us a while, but in the end there's more chance of us getting pregnant than not. Am I dreaming? I'm dreaming, aren't I?

He dragged me out of my reverie by firing acronyms at us.

QFG's ART options are these: you can have straight IVF, IVF with a touch of ICSI before your ET, AIH or maybe you'd like to go with GIFT? Of course if we experience any OHSS we may need to do an FET.

So. Have a think about those. What do you think?

That such potentially invasive and life-changing treatments could be boiled down to a single droplet of alphabet soup boggled my mind. *So, Doc, will we just SMS our answer in or what?*

With our minds on the verge of shutdown, Smith mentioned that the first step in our treatment was to finally establish exactly what state Liz's ovaries were in. She was booked in three days later for something called a laparoscopy. To me, a laparoscopy sounded like what a naughty nurse stripper gives the buck at a buck's party, but no, it was a distasteful procedure in which Liz would have a thin metal device with a camera on the end inserted into her innards through a tiny incision in her navel. We knew her ovaries were polycystic, but the doc needed to know just what state they were in and if she had any problems with her other reproductive organs. During the laparoscopy, while Liz was under a general anaesthetic, he would inspect Liz's ovaries and also check her tubes for blockages and her uterus for problems like endometriosis, a condition where the uterus lining is found outside the uterus. The presence of either of these conditions could affect what type of fertility treatment (ARTs: assisted reproductive technologies) would be suitable for us.

This led quickly to the next boom gate to negotiate on our winding road to parenthood—Liz's hospital phobia.

While the reason is unclear—she wasn't sickly as a child, and I'm not aware of any major hospital incidents that scarred her—Liz has never been comfortable among the medical establishment. Even a trip to a GP will set her stomach out of kilter, so the prospect of her innards being transformed into a TV studio under general anaesthesia was one she was not at all chuffed about. Thankfully, with only three days' notice, she didn't have time for the stress to build to epic proportions. At that point I estimated she was merely placed somewhere between extremely apprehensive and terrified witless.

After more than two years of marriage, it's fair to say that I was becoming more attuned to her moods. Now, when I found her sitting silently on the couch in the dark, tapping her foot and staring into space, I knew just what to say.

'Hey, you're not worried about this hospital thing are you?'

Worried was not quite the word. I think her logical brain had the sound bites 'It's going to be okay' and 'People have general anaesthetics all the time' playing on a loop, but the problem with your logical brain is that it speaks in that calm, quiet, monotone. It's too easily shouted down by the screaming, clawing, hair-pulling fiend that lives over in the irrational side of your mental duplex. If I put my head next to Liz's at night I swore I could actually hear it. It sounded a bit like *'OHSHITSOWHATIFONLYONEINFIVETHOUSANDDIEUNDERGENERALANAES THETICIFTHEPOORDEADFUCKERISMEEEEEE!'*

After a few attempts at comforting her, I worked out that there wasn't a lot I could say to allay her fears, so I concentrated on not mentioning it and finding other things to keep us busy for three days.

On the day of the laparoscopy, we parked underneath the swanky private medical centre and made our way up in the lift like we were ascending the Tower of London.

There wasn't much I could do other than offer a pained smile and rub Liz's back as she filled out paperwork and was briefed by the nurses on what to expect. Soon we said goodbye and I watched as my brave little soldier was led away, still managing to hold it together. A couple of hours later I was back in the recovery room patting the hand of my groggy, but still slightly panicked wife.

Aside from a delayed-reaction anxiety attack at the movies two days later and halfway through *Something's Gotta Give* (watching Keanu Reeves 'act' has forced many an unsuspecting cinema-goer to fight for breath and flee in terror over the years) everything had gone smoothly. I knew Liz still had deep reservations about hospital visits—she had a bruised belly button and small scar as physical evidence of their evil—but she'd coped well, at least on the outside. Perhaps the chatter in her head was telling another story, but I chose not to listen.

During our next appointment with Doctor Smith the results were more cause for celebration. The doc had found no tubes blocked, no endometriosis and no reproductive problems other than a pair of ovaries that displayed classic polycystic characteristics. They were swollen and dotted with cysts; the usual 'golf ball' appearance. As usual, Doctor Smith was upbeat and said the good news improved our choices and chances of conception.

So, okay. What acronymic option did we think we'd take?

On the spot for the first time, we muttered something about thinking it over and scuttled out the door, promising to get back to him.

IVF's various moral issues had crossed our radar screens before this point, and we had discussed some of them in passing in order to get this far, but it was about time we sat down and had a serious chat. With the telly off and everything. Any treatment option we took would have to be made with all the moral boxes ticked, and it was almost decision time.

When we first started our reproductive investigations, we soon saw the writing on the wall and devoured the ever-present IVF literature, so we knew vaguely what was involved in each assisted reproduction technique. The overriding ethical dilemma with all of them, as we saw it, was a fundamental one: is using any kind of ART 'playing God'? The way it seemed to us, with what we knew of the processes, God, Buddha, karma or any other cosmic belief system you'd like to burn incense to would still have a very big part to play. If we really weren't meant to have kids our embryos wouldn't form or wouldn't grow in Liz's womb and the universe would be satisfied. Although we might give the process a helping hand, there was still no way to conjure up that miraculous moment of conception in the womb. Clearly, at this point just leaving it to nature was unlikely to provide the result we were so desperate for, so we were happy to give nature all the help we could and then rely on her. But she still had to step in. If it happened, then it was meant to be.

We also felt more than a little justified in resorting to such high-tech tactics to give ourselves the best opportunity of having a baby. From what we had learned about modern foods, pesticides, cleaning products and other environmental factors degrading sperm and messing with women's systems, not to mention a suspected goodly dose of radiation courtesy of the Royal Australian Air Force, we were merely fighting fire with fire. If modern life was robbing us of our fertility, as declining sperm counts seem to prove, then we had no problem using the medical advances it afforded us to fight back.

Another decision that had to be made was what to do with any leftover embryos that we might produce. Even talking about it, our reaction to the words 'leftover', 'unneeded' or 'unused' was pretty indicative of how we felt. No matter how you said them they always sounded so ugly and cruel, like our would-be children were unwanted and just a product to be flushed like a dead goldfish. We quickly knew that, in the unlikely event that we produced scads of embryos, none would be discarded. They would all have their chance to latch on in the womb, even if that meant we'd end up with a cricket team of rugrats. We'd seen the literature begging for embryo donation to help couples who couldn't produce their own but, from where we sat at that point, we just couldn't do it. Should the shoe swap to the other foot and we were to find ourselves needing a donor embryo, well, we'd tear our hair out over that one another time.

The only other issue we considered was the emotional effect of IVF on any children it produced. This thought was both exciting and sobering at the same time. Kids! Us! It was intoxicating. But what if they felt different or strange about being created this way? To us, in 2004, it was no big deal—he, she or they would still be half me and half Liz and grow in her womb and be born like everyone else—but to kids little things can mean a lot. Would a little medical wizardry at the start of the process really worry him, her, them? We decided that, to a large extent, the answer to that question was up to us and how we handled the 'where did I come from' questions.

Liz had an ex-colleague who had had two IVF babies in the 'old days' when IVF pregnancies were a much rarer event. She told Liz that she had taught her kids that they were extra-special and the IVF process just meant that mum and dad had wanted them very, very much. This sounded like a good approach to us. Surely, with a stable home life and lots of love, it wouldn't prove to be too much of a stumbling block. I envisaged using a broken-arm analogy to help my little son/daughter understand.

If you break your arm you need a doctor's help to fix it, and there's nothing wrong with that, right? Your mum and I just had other parts broken that we needed a doctor's help with to make you.

Also, with IVF rates climbing dramatically, we were confident that our 'kids' really wouldn't feel that different anymore. The odds were that there'd be, on average, one ART child in every class when they got to school.

The only thing left to do was create them.

Medically, the jury was still out. For us the best options boiled down to a two-horse race.

Option 1: In-vitro fertilisation (IVF) is the classic 'test tube' technique. In a nutshell, it involves the female patient taking a course of drugs to force her ovaries to grow eggs at a specific time, and then harvesting the eggs through the abdomen or the vagina. Sperm is then collected from the male and added to the eggs in the lab in an effort to grow embryos. The chances of coming up with viable pre-humans can be further increased by having each egg manually injected with a single sperm, an optional extra known as ICSI—intra-cytoplasmic sperm injection.

Option 2: A kind of assisted artificial insemination (AIH: artificial insemination by husband) was the gentler, less invasive option. This technique would also employ a course of our old friend Clomid to help Liz's ovaries produce eggs, but since there is no harvesting of eggs for a later time, fewer are needed and therefore lower drug dosages are used. Sperm is then collected from the male, prepared and injected into the female's cervix in a non-surgical procedure. The rest of the process is left to occur naturally.

We to-ed and fro-ed with the decision many times. IVF involved more drugs, and an egg harvesting operation (EPU: egg pick-up) that probably meant another general anaesthetic and incision in the navel for Liz. Given her fear of all things medical, it was not the ideal solution, but on the plus side the doctor said that our chance of conceiving with an IVF 'cycle' would be around 50 per cent. The odds were much lower with artificial insemination—somewhere between 20 and 30 per cent. Was it worth toughing out what would undoubtedly be a traumatic hospital experience for Liz in the hope that it would take fewer cycles for a positive result? What if a couple of assisted AIH cycles, with low hospital stress, would do the trick? A lot of pain, expense and unnecessary drugs could be avoided, but it's a false economy if the treatment doesn't work...

When we left Dr Smith's rooms we were pretty sure the assisted AIH was the option for us. If Liz couldn't cope with the hospital procedures associated with IVF, well that was our decision made right there. We'd just persist with 'IVF lite' for as long as it took, and if that meant a couple of years of trying and doctors' bills, we'd live under that bridge when we came to it.

But what if she could somehow get through an EPU (egg pick-up)? What if she fell pregnant first go? Even if we weren't that lucky, the extra eggs collected in the first cycle could be frozen (FET: frozen embryo transfer) and we could have three or four more cycles worth of eggs in the bank—no EPUs required.

The monetary considerations were secondary, but still a factor. Medicare rebates, Medicare Safety Net and health fund coverage taken into account, we would be out of pocket more than $3000 for each IVF cycle, with drugs costs on top of that, while assisted AIH would cost about $1500 per cycle including drugs.

The folk at Queensland Fertility Group were quite conscientious in giving us a fee schedule for each of the main assisted reproductive technology options, but it's not possible to predict the overall cost of treatment because it can vary with the individual. One woman may respond to a lower drug dosage than another; one may need an extra procedure. Adding to the confusion were the government's cryptic rebate schemes. QFG could quote exact procedure and drug costs, but no-one was quite sure what kind of rebate you would get from whom. Many were the early-morning discussions had at the QFG nurses' station trying to figure out what would be the final damage. We were dealing with more gaps than a backwoods orthodontist.

Me (handing over cash): 'Hi. The doctor says we need some Synarel nasal spray, and 60 progesterone pessaries, thanks.'

Nurse 1: 'Here you go. That's $290, please.'

Nurse 2: 'Now, don't forget to take this receipt to Medicare.'

Me: 'I thought drug receipts went to private health funds...'

Nurse 2: 'I think you'll get something from Medicare but you can also try the gap with your fund, just don't forget to check the schedule limit. Who are you with?'

Me: 'Medibank Private.'

Nurse 1: 'Actually, I'm not sure if Medibank Private are reimbursing for pessaries if we dispense them. We're still waiting on accreditation. But the Medicare Safety Net will help out. Now, how much did you give me?'

A couple of months after our first visit, we were back in front of Dr Smith singing an IVF tune. Bravely, Liz had decided that she would try to manage her fear and take on an IVF cycle. I was secretly leaning toward this option during the decision-making process, but was careful not to let my bias show. Given that the sum total of my hardship would be wanking into a jar, I didn't think I had too many votes on this particular jury. Ironically, I have no fear of hospitals and, if our positions could have been reversed, would have jumped at the chance to take over the being-harvested duties but, of course, this was of no comfort to Liz.

Coming from the 'shock and awe' school of fertility treatment, I could tell IVF was the option the doc was keenest on for us. It was right up his alley: plenty of drugs, immediate maximum impact, best odds. Once the decision was made, however, Liz faced the prospect of a long course of drugs, an egg pick-up and the chance of ovarian hyperstimulation syndrome. OHSS occurs after women with PCOS undergo a course of follicle stimulating hormones (FSH) to stimulate the ovaries into producing eggs at a specified time. Polycystic ovaries can respond excessively to this stimulation and produce large numbers of eggs and therefore release large amounts of their own hormones. Because the ovaries are larger than normal to begin with, when they swell further and release large amounts of fluids, problems can occur. Symptoms of mild OHSS include abdominal pain and nausea, but in rare cases severe dehydration can lead to hospitalisation. There are even very rare cases of patients dying from OHSS.

As Smith related this latest batch of stats, the room went quiet, the only sound a familiar tiny voice screaming, '*VERYVERYRAREBUTIFYOU'RETHERAREDEADONETHENITAIN'TSOFRIGGIN RAREISITSMARTGUY!*' I looked over at my wife, but her face was a calm sea of determination. We locked it in.

The first thing we did was book in for a session with the centre's in-house psychologist.

If we were going to put ourselves (by 'ourselves' I mean Liz) through a battery of medical tests, injections and operations with a view to a pregnancy, which would involve us (by 'us' I mean Liz) living through even more tests and jabs and the painful bit at the end, Liz needed help with her panic attacks and I needed help with my empathy skills.

Our psychologist was tall, thin and suitably mad-professor-like, with a shock of white, wiry hair either side of a bald central pate. Perhaps I walked into the session on the defensive, but I was quite surprised that he seemed to speak a lot of sense. He helped Liz with some techniques to deal with her panic attacks and even established that she might have a very mild case of asthma. She had been mistaking this for hyperventilation, and struggling for breath had been escalating her panic.

The prof talked to me about remembering that everyone is different. Just because I don't fear hospitals, it is a very valid, normal fear for many people, and of course it was okay for Liz to worry about it. I remembered that I am afraid of public speaking, whereas Liz can stand up and speak in front of anyone.

'Liz's fear is like a kick in the balls,' he said.

'I'm sorry?'

'You know what a kick in the balls feels like?'

'Of course,' I said. 'My pick-up lines were some of the worst going around.'

'Okay,' said the prof, 'so how would you describe that feeling to Liz? What's it feel like?'

'Well...um, it's unique—hard to describe. It doesn't take much force, but it can drop you like a stone...'

'And for a woman who had never seen that, it'd be very hard to believe a little touch could do that, wouldn't it?'

'Yes it would.'

'So just think of Liz's fear as her own personal kick in the balls.'

On the eve of our first cycle of IVF, I realised later that it was a masterful analogy.

On the home front, the kitchen cupboards were filled but the social cupboards were bare. A nice house is a great start, but we had no jobs, no friends and no long-term means to feed our mortgage monster, as manageable and cuddly as he was.

Part of the reason for our move was to have the financial flexibility for both of us to work part-time. I could always fall back on writing freelance stories for mags and newspapers I'd worked for, but for Liz the move meant an opportunity to dip her toe into the waters of a new career. As a primary school teacher for nine years, she had effectively been in school since the age of five and had never had the opportunity to get herself grubby in the private sector. She desperately needed a change.

For weeks we scanned the careers lift-out in the Saturday paper, looking for opportunities that would suit. Since her many and varied skills all revolved around the one career she needed a break from, it was a challenge finding something in which she could start from scratch.

She applied for jobs as a clerk, an admin assistant, a real estate agent and a blackjack dealer and many things in between, but with skills and experience in the wrong field, the going was tough. There were few callbacks and even fewer interviews. It was about as promising as a rain dance on the moon.

We had lowered our sights to casual call-centre work when Liz got a call for a mass interview at Brisbane's Treasury Casino. From 300 applicants, in March 2004 Liz was chosen as one of 40 trainees to learn the mystical art of dealing blackjack. She had wanted something completely different and it would certainly tick that box.

While I was lollygagging around in slippers and trakkie daks working from home during the day, Liz was rising at 5.30am for a seven o'clock start at the casino. Her evenings were spent standing at the dining table practising her dealing, hand-positioning or chip-stacking on a green blackjack felt. It was a slow process, sometimes involving tears of frustration and pep talks from yours truly, but eventually her technique was spot-on and her speed was up to par. After four weeks of unpaid full-time training, at the ripe old age of 30, the schoolteacher I shared my bed with had transformed herself into a worldly-wise casual blackjack dealer, capable of holding her own in any casino on the planet.

In the meantime I had wormed my way into shifts of casual sub-editing on the news desk at the *Courier-Mail*. I must have done okay, because fill-in shifts for sick staff soon turned into a regular few days of work on the news and sports sections. Financially, we'd fallen on our feet with enough work to keep us comfortable and not frantic. After all, the whole point of the interstate exercise was to shift our workloads back a few gears, for fertility's sake.

On the other side of the balance sheet, this part-time, lackadaisical lifestyle doesn't entirely gel with IVF treatment. There were bills to pay. Big bills. Confusing bills. Pay-the-doctor-a-fat-cheque-upfront-and-the-big-government-agency-will-send-you-a-random-rebate-cheque -six-weeks-later kind of bills. Money was soon gushing out of our account and being funnelled to doctors, clinics, Medicare, Medibank Private and sometimes back again. Liz, with her big-picture brain, could somehow keep track of the Gordian knot of money-flow and instinctively knew what receipts we should shove in front of whom and when. I, the details man, was utterly frustrated and overwhelmed by the whole process.

Medically, our IVF cycle was in full swing before we knew it. Game on, baby!

The first step for Liz was a goodly snort of Synarel, a drug that blocked Liz's own unpredictable hormones and provided the docs with a level playing field. This was delivered via an unpleasant shot of nasal spray a couple of times a day. After a couple of weeks of this she started a daily series of hormone (FSH) injections to spur her ovaries into producing eggs. We had been trained by the nurse in the use of a nifty little pen-like syringe with which she jabbed herself in the abdomen every morning. Its needle was very fine, and despite Liz's medical issues she was a trouper. Every morning she would lay out her syringe, needle and sharps bin, fit the needle, dial up the correct dose, look away and plunge it in, careful to get her skin's tension just right so the good stuff didn't leak out again.

It seemed a little odd—on one hand blocking Liz's God-given hormones from taking effect while pumping her full of the synthetic variety in the next breath. Still ... doctor's orders. Doctor's orders also included turning up at the QFG medical centre for regular blood tests to check her hormone levels.

While Liz was in a small room trying not to look at the big needle sucking blood from her arm, I spent some of my time examining the pegboards dotted through-out the centre. They were crammed with hundreds of overlapping baby-shaped images cut from photographs obviously sent in by a host of delirious and thankful parents. Babies of all different colours and sizes lay there frozen in mid-gurgle, squark or wince, some fresh from the womb and held by doctors, others alone in cots, still others held by smiling older siblings, sometimes in pairs or even threes. As I smiled at the comical faces and sheer cuteness of this battalion of tots, these 'vanity boards' struck me as a testament to man's medical skill. Much later I realised that, more than medical ingenuity, they were a testament to the single-mindedness and determination of the children's parents.

As I browsed the rows of chubby faces I always felt a pang of jealousy and wondered if we would ever add our own photo to those legions of unsullied innocence hanging proudly on QFG's walls.

As the weeks passed, we increased the hormone levels on Liz's syringe and readied ourselves for the business end of the cycle: eggs, sperm and, fingers crossed, healthy embryos.

When she wasn't using her belly as a dartboard, Liz was at Treasury Casino, dealing cards to an endless stream of punters at all hours of the day and night. At home, the clue that she was up to speed, skill-wise, was when she would pass the salt at dinner and then automatically flick her palm over to display 'clean hands', just in case there was any question she was stealing pinches to sell on the seasoning black market.

The casino ran three eight-hour shifts around the clock and, although every effort was supposed to be made to give staff regular hours, Liz found herself working across all three shifts (day shift: 12pm–8pm; swing shift: 8pm–4am; graveyard shift: 4am–12pm). As day shifts were the most popular among long-time employees, new graduates were left to nominate for either graveyard or swing shift, but a staffing foul-up meant that Liz's course ended up working a combination of both. This was not a big issue for most of her graduating class of nineteen- and twenty-year-olds living a party lifestyle, but Liz was one of only a handful that had kissed their mid-twenties goodbye and was yearning for some body clock stability for medical reasons. The situation was not ideal. The stress of performing under pressure coupled with the possible implications of the vague smell of smoke on the 'smoke-free' casino floor, being on her feet for long periods and the horrendous hours were quickly eating away at our lifestyle seachange.

Still, her shift work meant she was usually free during the day for amusing diversions such as medical appointments, operations and general anaesthesia.

By May, Liz had absorbed enough drugs to grow her eggs for the egg pick-up. During another cheery session with Doctor Smith, using an ultrasound wand and a handful of goo he discovered Liz had at least 14–16 eggs on her ovaries ready to pop, and we were booked in for the crucial operation. Like a toilet paper streamer stuck to your shoe, the egg pick-up dragged with it a distasteful little item: another general anaesthetic.

At a carefully calculated moment that just happened to be three in the morning the night before the EPU, we were to inject Liz with a last belt of hormones, which would cause her eggs to mature at precisely the right time for the operation.

We drove into the day theatre carpark and waved to the attendant. It felt like we'd seen more of that guy than we had of our immediate relatives during the medical boot camp we'd been stuck in over the previous three months. Not counting Liz's laparoscopy, we were two months into the IVF cycle and were keener to see its resolution with every passing day. As we sat in the waiting room I squeezed Liz's hand and wished for the kajillionth time that I could do more. Her breathing was measured and she looked in control so I left it at that and flicked through my trashy magazine.

We were ushered into a small briefing room where a kindly, experienced nurse told us what we could expect from the surgery. Once Liz was prepped and under general anaesthetic, Doctor Smith would stride in and insert a tiny vaginal ultrasound probe with a needle in its head into her. This would enable him to find the follicles growing on Liz's ovaries and use the needle to suck the fluid from them. An IVF scientist would then sort through the fluid and set aside the eggs.

When the time came for Liz to be led away, I managed to get a hug in but she didn't want to get too emotional. She was in the zone.

Soon it was my turn. I had to provide the other half of the equation.

There, in the hospital, in the next half an hour please, Mister Davis.

The hospital staff didn't call it The Wank Room and there was no handy 'This way to The Wank Room' signage, but that's precisely what it was. As wank rooms go, though, it was evident a good deal of effort had gone into the design and construction of this particular ejaculatory conservatory. This was a room designed to enhance its occupants' organ-playing experience as much as humanly possible.

As instructed I fronted up to the nurses' station and, in a barely audible mumble, asked for 'the key'.

'How will they know what key I'm talking about?' I'd asked during the briefing.

'Oh, they'll know,' the nurse replied.

They knew all right, but it was not as easy as slapping the counter and ordering a McHappy Meal. I could barely squeak out the words. To their credit, the nurses were obviously fluent in gibber, for they knew precisely what I was after. And, I presumed, what I was going to do with it, and myself, when I got there. But they're nurses, right? And it's just a natural body function. They wouldn't even bat an eyelid, right? It's just that I'm doing it for strangers. On a schedule.

A nurse handed over the key in question and carefully explained that *there was only one*. Did I understand? There were no copies. I understood perfectly. Directions to the room were clearly and discreetly explained, and all with a complete absence of smirking and eyelid-batting. The batting would commence momentarily.

On a different floor I found an unmarked door that could have been a broom cupboard or electrical junction box, but the key in my hand fitted, so I stepped inside quickly, closed the door behind me, checked it was locked and checked it again.

I turned around, and suddenly I was Maxwell Smart on my way in to Control. Ahead was a long corridor, with another door at the end and a room beyond. I locked the second door, tested the handle and finally took a breath. It was an ideal pud-pulling environment. Ask any sixteen-year-old boy what his number one requirement for a good hand shandy session is and, if he's honest, he'll say 'security', before he spontaneously combusts with embarrassment. If you have to keep an eye out in case your mum bursts through the door of your room, you just ain't gonna perform.

The room looked like a converted doctor's room: carpet on the floor, a washbasin in one corner, linen basket in the other, a bank of well-frosted windows. What set it apart from any other doctor's rooms I've encountered is the daybed and throw-cushions against one wall, the TV/video stocked with porn and the large sign on the wall that asked everyone to 'PLEASE CHANGE ANY SOILED LINEN ON DAYBEAD. THIS IS FOR THE HYGIENE AND COMFORT OF OTHERS.' It's a glamorous affair, this IVF.

Like all good wank rooms, this one came with plenty of instructions. Another informative piece of signage spelled out the rules of the room, mainly concerned with cleanliness, neatness and the collection of samples. Ah, yes. There was a hefty supply of my old friend the yellow-lidded plastic jar on the window sill, and I was to fill out the label carefully, including my name, date of birth and, most importantly, the time of sample collection. There were even paper bags to disguise your sample for the trip back up to the nurses. It was all most agreeable, as far as these things went. Well thought out, secure and reasonably comfortable, if slightly creepy.

I checked the doors again, sat on the daybed and searched for inspiration.

Soon enough I was back upstairs delivering my care package. When I dropped it off I remembered a fleeting moment earlier in the day when I'd seen another guy pass a paper bag across the counter. At the time I'd thought he was a courier or somebody's husband bringing in one of the nurses' lunch.

An hour later I was by Liz's side in the recovery ward. She lay there in her curtained-off area, pale, groggy and wearing an oxygen mask across the same determined stare she'd gone in with. I tried to stroke her arm, but she gently brushed it aside. She was trying to hold it together and didn't need the distraction. Her breathing was laboured and she was shivering. I stood there keeping a close eye on her, and made myself useful by shifting from foot to foot, looking around the room anxiously and conscientiously worrying about anything I could think of.

Liz slowly improved and eventually was well enough for a nurse to bring a phone to the bedside. Doctor Smith was on the line to relay the brilliant news that Liz had produced a whopping twenty eggs, more than enough to be going on with. He said scientists were scurrying around brandishing test tubes and incubators at that very moment, adding my sperm to those fresh eggs and, as usual, he was supremely confident. Soon we'd be the proud owners of a bevy of bouncing embryos. Very soon, technically, depending on whom you believe, we'd be able to consider ourselves parents.

LIFE EXPECTANCY

Our next visit to Doctor Smith brought big news, both good and bad. Good in that we had six viable, healthy, dividing embryos just waiting for a place to grow, and bad because their next port of call would have to be the deep freeze—Liz was a good bet to suffer ovarian hyper-stimulation (OHSS) if we went any further immediately.

Liz had produced a mammoth twenty eggs from a pair of already painfully swollen ovaries, and during the egg pick-up the doc confirmed that they were ready for a rest. Twenty eggs was roughly four more than Doctor Smith had expected, and her polycystic ovaries put her at a higher risk of serious OHSS symptoms if we were to carry on and pump her full of still more hormones.

The doc called a month-long break to the process to give Liz's ovaries time to recover and us time to dwell on things. It meant another frustrating delay to our progress.

Using ICSI (intra-cytoplasmic sperm injection) to inject every one of Liz's eggs with one of my wrigglers (I always imagine this process occurring in a warm Petri dish of the ilk we used to use in Mrs Wadsworth's chemistry class) the scientists had come up with six strong embryos with cells that had divided in the lab. All in all, Doctor Smith admitted that six from twenty was a disappointing result, but it was enough for between three and six cycles of IVF.

Were we disappointed? Yes—no argument there. During the sugar-coating period of our five-minute consultation, a joke occurred to me in an...erm...light-bulb moment.

Q: How many IVF scientists does it take to change a light bulb?

A: One, but he'll need ten to get one to work.

On relaying the news our doctor came up with platitudes such as 'well, these things just happen' and 'that's plenty of embryos really' and 'at least they're healthy'. The truth is that no-one can say why some eggs fertilise and some don't, and to not have the answers on hand was so far outside the 'control everything' ethos of IVF that it just didn't compute. I wanted to stamp my foot and hold my breath until I turned blue, or go and shake someone until they came up with an explanation. Then I thought about the couples who end up sitting in my place hearing they have one or (God forbid) no chance at a baby.

There was more news. Apparently we'd had seven embryos to start with, but one was not deemed 'viable'—

that is, its cells were fragmented and it had little or no chance of survival if frozen or implanted in the womb.

So what is the appropriate response to *this* little titbit? Do we mourn the loss of a potential child, or consider that non-viable embryos, which die in the womb during normal conception, are part of the natural process too? In any case, in Doctor Smith's office there is no time to sit around and contemplate your navel. We treated ourselves to a short period of freezing like deer in the headlights until we were ushered out the door to let the waves of unprocessable information wash over us.

And we had other pressing issues to worry about—making sure Liz didn't suffer too much with hyperstimulation. We were on the lookout for symptoms of serious OHSS, although we soon discovered there's a fine line between vigilance and unbridled mania.

The situation was reminiscent of that sequence from *Aliens* where Ripley wakes up in a safe, comfy hospital bed and everything is hunky-dory, until she looks down to see her friendly neighbourhood xenomorph doing an Austrian polka under the skin of her belly. You might recall that Ripley was only dreaming at the time, but over the next two weeks we shared her nightmare. As the days passed, Liz found that the pain from the operation faded but was replaced by something else. Slowly, surely, her belly was growing and becoming increasingly taut and uncomfortable. As predicted, the fluid lost into Liz's innards when her ovaries' many egg follicles burst to release their eggs was causing problems.

During the first few days after the operation, Liz treated herself to a break from fleecing punters at the casino and just took it easy around the house. She was reduced to lounging on the couch in voluminous trakkie daks and rubbing her slightly swollen abdomen as the considerable pain that comes from having a probe twiddled around in your insides gradually faded and was replaced by mere general discomfort. I chimed in with a morale-boosting 'no worries' and consigned her swollen belly to my mental out box. The pain was fading, problem solved—let's move on.

But the problem remained. The swelling didn't go away. In fact, as feared, her belly grew, slowly, insidiously, and the discomfort in her abdomen remained as the follicles on her ovaries continued to leak fluid into her innards and slowly turn her into a human bongo drum. She was doing all the right things but, ten days after the egg pick-up, the bloating around her middle was no better. Rather than cutting back on food and water in the face of the bloating—this only exacerbates the symptoms—she had been advised to increase her protein intake and water consumption to replace the fluid she'd lost. With a pressure-cooker abdomen this task was far from easy. The last thing Liz wanted to do was stuff herself full of still more fluid and hearty protein-based meals. But she did it. She was doing all the right things.

And yet, two weeks post-operation and the bloating was showing no signs of abating. She said working helped keep her mind off it but, worse than the tenderness were the constant nagging questions: when is this going to go away, or will it get worse?

Normally as cool, calm and considered as the Victorian Police Force on cracker night, I found it was enough to make me twitch. The medicos couldn't tell us how big my wife's belly was going to get, we certainly had no clue, and the fluid baby wasn't talking, so where did that leave us?

It left us, once again, waiting and worrying. As we entered the third week after her EPU, I'd broken my own rule and started scouring the internet for alarming misinformation and Liz had relented and rung the nurses for reassurance. We read more about the rare cases of OHSS hospitalisations and (*gulp*) deaths and quietly flipped out.

Then, over the next few days, her belly peaked. A week later the swelling had abated and the drama along with it. We were left checking her belly, laughing nervously and marvelling at how fast it had subsided.

Soon my wife was back in good form, and I know this because she had started to give me a hard time again. Business as usual at Casa del Davis.

The whole saga, three weeks' recovery time and a three-week wait until the middle of Liz's next cycle, afforded us a six-week break from IVF—time enough for a good think, several lengthy bouts of morbid self-defeatism and the odd spurt of lashing out at inanimate objects.

Far from an opportunity to get a bit of distance on the whole drama, for me all the break achieved was to put a dent in my self-resolve and dredge up unproductive questions about fate and the meaning of life.

What if our dream of children just wasn't meant to be? Even worse, what if there was a *reason* we weren't falling naturally? Sure, the PCOS and low sperm count weren't helping, but what if there was a more cosmic reason? What if the natural world was trying to tell us something and we were bucking the order of things by not leaving well enough alone? We'd already had the discussion about kids with physical or mental disabilities and we had steadfastly resolved to raise any children we were blessed with, come what may, but my overactive imagination was trotting other possibilities across the back of my mind, each one more disturbing than the last. I wondered about the course the twentieth century might have taken had, for example, Mr and Mrs Hitler been on the borderline for achieving conception.

Yes, this is what happens in my head when there is nothing decent on TV.

About the same time, we had the other discussion that pregnancy-challenged couples have: adoption. We both agreed that we would apply to adopt a child if all else failed, but we were nowhere near a consensus when it came to the details. Because there is traditionally more demand for very young babies, Liz—in yet another example of her selflessness—said she would be happy to adopt a child of up to five years old. I, on the other hand, knew I would want a newborn, preferably a pale, WASPy one like we are. I figured that might help to ease the burden of self-doubt that must nag kids who look different from their parents, and remove the awkward moments and playground teasing that they must endure. And, if I'm honest, I probably just wanted one that looked like me to forget the failure of not being able to produce our own.

But we weren't even approaching the on-ramp to that bridge yet, so we left these issues and their tiny attached red flags for another, even less happy time. The adoption question, however, brought with it a distasteful companion, sort of like your favourite cousin and her leg-humping cocker spaniel Thrusty Rusty. How long would we wait before giving up on IVF? We had 5–10 years in us before the fertility gods would frown on us even more than they already had, but I doubted whether we had the mental fortitude to last that long. What we'd been through already was soul-destroying enough. A solid ten-year stint of IVF would take an almost unimaginable toll emotionally, physically and financially.

Eventually we agreed we'd give it a loose mid-range time period of three to five years before taking another look at our options. They were arbitrary figures, really. Clearly there was no way to judge how disconsolate each new roadblock would make us, and at the rate cycle one was going I secretly wondered if we'd even see cycle two.

By July the spectre of OHSS had passed, but it had done nothing to ease Liz's fears of all things medical and pharmaceutical and the effects the process was having on her body. She had physically recovered from her hyperstimulation, but I was worried the episode had damaged her mental resolve to withstand the rigours still to come. How many cycles could she stand? It's easy to say we could keep going for five years but on current evidence, realistically I put it at more like three cycles. Four at the outside. Again, there was no way to tell, and no way to raise the issue without coming off as either pushy or unsupportive. One thing we had already learned from our first cycle was that all the planning in the world counted for naught when pitted against the curve balls the process could throw at you. There was nothing for it but to cross our fingers and focus on the next thing.

This being the delicate, finely tuned twenty-first-century process it was, the next thing was a whacking great course of drugs you couldn't jump over. The doc had to wait until Liz was in the middle of her theoretical cycle before resuming our treatment, known as a 'thaw cycle' because the embryos are being pulled out of the deep freeze, thawed and thrust into the womb. To pave the way for the embryos and mimic the natural state of the body at ovulation, Liz started a course of oestrogen tablets which encouraged the lining of the uterus to thicken and thus aided implantation of our microscopic munchkin. Over the next ten days, Liz popped her pills morning and night and I wondered about our embryos. Although rates of successful embryo thawing in modern IVF are very high and embryos that are not robust are not frozen in the first place, what if our one little fella was the one in a squillion that didn't emerge from the Arctic tundra unscathed?

An ultrasound scan from Doctor Smith soon confirmed Liz's uterine wall was thick enough and he gave us a prescription for progesterone pessaries to get it even more plump and ready for implantation. I had no idea what a pessary was until we shelled out for a big bag of 60 foil-wrapped conical 'lollies' at the QFG nurses' station. They looked a bit like little squashed Easter eggs and I wondered if they would taste chalky or if the manufacturers had given them a flavour.

Soon the light bulb clicked on. Hormone... delivered to the right area... conical shape...

As we paid for our bag of lollies I leaned close to Liz's ear and waggled my index finger in an embarrassing manner. 'So you have to shove them up...'

She shot me a withering look. 'You got it. Yet another indignity for the womenfolk, darling.'

And you have to pay $3 a pop for the privilege, I thought. *Harsh.*

It was true, the whole process had hardly been fair. With my sperm possibly bearing more than half the blame for our infertility on their little sperm shoulders, all that had been asked of me was a couple of undignified sessions of polishing the dolphin. Meanwhile Liz had been sliced, diced, poked, prodded, knocked out, drugged up and harvested from. I often felt guilty about the extra medical burden she had to endure, especially given the fact that she detested anything involving blood, scalpels, probes or anaesthetic. Every time she had faced another stint on a hospital bed or examination table, I wished we could swap places so that I could have spared her the discomfort but, more than that, doing a few hard yards under the knife also would have gone some way toward assuaging my guilt. If it had turned out that I had been the sole cause of our infertility, I don't know how I could have looked her in the eye. Perversely, occasionally I could even admit to myself that I was a little glad she had polycystic ovaries. And then I would feel guilty about that. And so it went.

As it was, with my sperm questionable at best and catatonic at worst, Liz never lashed out at me or even once swung the bony finger of blame my way. The worst I ever got was the odd gentle, wistful reminder—as with my short course in pessary manipulation—that, yes, I should think myself lucky.

Back in the dawn of time—by now more than three months previously—we had talked to Doctor Smith about transferring multiple embryos, survival rates and complications associated with multiple births. With the advances in IVF technology in Australia, patients are vigorously discouraged from transferring more than two embryos in a single IVF cycle. Research has proven that the practice of transferring three or more embryos results in pregnancy rates no higher than those achieved by transferring two. In addition, it exposes the patient to the possibility of giving birth to triplets or quads and the much greater mortality risks that high-order multiple births bring. So there was really only one decision to be made: whether to transfer one or two. After reading up on the statistics and finding that twins suffered a significantly higher risk of complications, certain abnormalities and infant mortality, we had decided to transfer one embryo only.

Doctor Smith told us that the pregnancy rates for transferring one and two embryos were virtually the same.

What would we do—go for the whole enchilada at once? If we got lucky with twins, we thought maybe two children would be enough for us and therefore we wouldn't have to go through another emotionally, physically and financially draining cycle. But that was a long shot, and would leave us with the dilemma of what to do with our remaining embryos. In the fantasy world I live in when this world starts to get too taxing, I imagined myself, the proud dad, outside the delivery room holding a towel-wrapped bundle of joy in the crook of each arm and grinning like a Lotto winner. Then I thought about Liz and me cutting a swathe through pedestrian traffic in a double-wide stroller stocked with identical blonde tots. It had a kind of daunting-but-wholesome *Brady Bunch* feel to it.

But the big decisions don't get made in la-la land.

In reality Liz and I quickly looked at the odds of complication and the added strain of twins, and it was a decision quickly made. Neither of us needed to talk the other around. It was hard to ignore the numbers and we'd reached the conclusion independently. We were hell-bent on doing anything and everything we could to improve the chances of our baby being healthy and happy, so a single transfer it would be. My double-birth dream life evaporated quickly under the harsh glare of risk and probability, but it was no great loss. A double miracle seemed about as far-fetched as a single one at that point.

The day before the transfer Liz decided to ring Doctor Smith's rooms to check that they were ready to thaw our embryo for the following day. I rolled my eyes and told her not to worry. We were dealing with health care professionals here, specialists in their fields no less, and if they couldn't organise shit from clay, well, where would we be? But Liz was just after some reassurance, so she called anyway. It was worth feeling a bit foolish. The most important thing was that it all went off without a hitch.

When Liz rang Doctor Smith's rooms she had an almost apologetic tone in her voice. Would it be okay if she checked that our embryo was ready? Elizabeth Davis... a transfer booked for tomorrow...

The news was as shocking as it was worrying. Our best embryos—they are ranked in terms of quality—had been frozen in 'straws' of two. In total, our six precious bundles of cells were frozen in four straws; the best four in two groups of two and the other two in single straws.

'Of course,' the secretary informed Liz, 'there's no way to thaw only one embryo in a straw of two, Mrs Davis.'

Liz paled and dropped the phone into its cradle.

It was difficult to push aside the shock and indignation we felt and logically plot the best course of action. It was the first time we'd ever been told of the existence of 'straws' and freezing in pairs, so this was a talk we hadn't had. We were, however, getting good at medical decision-making on the fly.

First off, we already knew that, after what we'd been through, there was no way we would be wasting any embryos. If we'd spent that amount of time, energy and money producing inanimate objects such as, say, bank tellers, we would think twice about discarding them, so we were certainly going to give all our thawed embryos a shot at the womb. I doubted QFG would let us waste them anyway. So the question now was, would we lead off with our best embryos or have the medicos thaw one of our lesser single embryos? If the process took several years, we might be better off with high-quality embryos left up our sleeves when Liz was a few years older. Or we could chuck our good eggs in her one basket now.

The options were clear-cut—an all-out assault versus a long-term strategy—but there was only one realistic choice. Since we'd started the process we had constantly been told how lucky we were that Liz was young enough that her age hadn't begun to be a big factor. Fertility doctors and nurses are forever warning patients not to leave it too long before investigating assisted fertility, because the clock is ticking. Loudly. Given that women's fertility at 35 is said to be half what it was at twenty, and it quickly tails off from there, we quickly realised that, whatever we were going to do, we'd better do it quickly and use the best of the resources we had.

And that's what we did.

We're picking our best team and playing every game like it's a final, I thought. We'd go with our two best eggs and would just have to swallow the extra risks that the possibility of twins carries with it. If we transferred two embryos, local stats suggested that we had about an 18 per cent chance of having twins.

We passed this re-made decision on to our doctor and associated scientists through gritted teeth. No-one likes being in the mailroom when the board of Your Life Pty Ltd meets, and much later we worked out how we'd been left out of the loop. When our cycle had been interrupted because of OHSS, we'd been sent home to recover without going through the standard procedure of discussing embryos, straws and how many of one to freeze in the other. When we picked up the reins again, it was all a done deal. The system had broken down and our precious embryos had been frozen arbitrarily.

Someone had simply made the decision for us. As you do.

Shove-The-Embryo-In Day may not sound as romantic as Valentine's Day or as hand-over-the-heart inspiring as, say, Norway Kipper Day, but if everything went as planned, we'd happily whip up some tickertape and throw our own parade.

As we cruised into the day surgery underground carpark and waved to our man 'Barry' the attendant, we again felt like we were stepping into battle. On our side was the fact that the procedure was non-surgical this time and involved no anaesthetic. A mere plastic tube-like transfer device would be inserted into my wife vaginally to deliver the two embryos into her womb—an undeniable walk in the park compared to last time we graced the green halls of the facility, but surely an unpleasant experience nonetheless.

This time the enemy was the fear again brought to the fore by the embryo mix-up: if the medical powers that be couldn't get the storage right, what other mistakes were lurking in the test tubes? Would our embryos be okay? Would they even be *our* embryos? By the time we ventured into the day surgery for the third time we had turned worrying into, if not an art form, certainly a semi-professional pastime.

On the ward, the nurses grabbed us and gave us the standard preparatory spiel—what would happen when to whom. I was surprised to be given the option of going with Liz into the operating theatre, and jumped at the chance. It would be a weird sensation, decked out in green paper clothes and standing by as several strangers set about placing our embryos inside my long-suffering wife, but I had been there at every other juncture and by the set line of her jaw I could tell she needed as much moral support as possible. And, if the truth be known, I was also just plain curious as to how the whole thing worked. As usual, I tried to make light of the situation to subliminally suggest to Liz that the procedure was no big deal which, as usual, was counterproductive. The way she saw it, I was suggesting that she was worrying over nothing.

Before we knew it we were both shut into a tiny room barely bigger than a cupboard, pulling green backless paper smocks off shelves. Liz put hers on in place of the comfy clothes she'd been advised to wear, and I put mine on over the top of mine. Soon we were both resplendent in hats, smocks and booties, ready for a fill-in shift hacking up carcasses at the nearest abattoir if the whole embryo thing didn't pan out. Of course, Liz would have been the only one on the production line with her bum showing.

From the change room, we stepped into the theatre. In the vast white room two banks of electronic instrumentation dominated the space, towering over an operating table, the core of the scene baked by a white-hot overhead light. The flashing lights, serpentine cables and towering machinery were like something out of a Terry Gilliam techno-nightmare. One of the nurses produced a low stool on wheels and I positioned myself next to the table on which my wife was arranging herself. Then the nurses rigged up a large green sheet on a frame that separated her top half from the fiddly, squidgy end and blocked both of our views. Hallelujah.

I sat beside Liz with her legs in the air and her crotch under lights and smiled politely as our nurse and scientist made breezy small talk as if we were chatting over tea and Scrabble. God only knows what I muttered, or where I eventually directed my gaze. Liz was in the zone again, so she was incommunicado, and I tired quickly of the machine that goes 'ping'. From where I sat the only actual action was centred at a side bench where the scientist was fussing over something I couldn't see.

There was no sign of the doctor yet, and I was just starting to wonder whether perhaps our procedure had clashed with his busy scowling-at-people schedule, when a door flew open and a masked man fitting his description strode in in mid-sentence and stuck on fast-forward. He was dashing about as if he had fifteen transfers to do in the next hour. With his workload, maybe he did. As usual, his self-important air was maddening, and yet somehow also intensely annoying.

He offered us some perfunctory greetings, then took a thin plastic probe-like device from the scientist and disappeared from view behind the sheet. Less than 60 seconds later Liz released a breath and Doctor Smith announced he was finished.

Transfer done, two embryos in and not a Petri dish or a Bunsen burner in sight.

I helped Liz off the table and we changed back in the tiny anteroom. Was it my imagination or was she walking a little...carefully? It must have been an odd feeling to think that two of the living things we'd spent so much effort producing were just sitting there inside her, deciding whether to latch on or just wink out of existence.

In the recovery room, we hit the comfy chairs again and were just submitting to the TV mind-suck when something odd happened. One of the nurses offered Liz a shot of brandy for her nerves. This, the woman who had barely had a drink in twelve months, was being poured a goodly-sized snort of the hard stuff by a medical professional at precisely the moment that she'd begun teetering on the brink of pregnancy. Still, when the nurse says 'jump', you say, 'How beaut. Lesh get snozzled.' Liz tipped it down the hatch and the colour returned to her face. I wonder whether this technique has any medical benefit; perhaps someone just happened to go through duty-free that week.

We sat, rested and tried to stop our minds from whirring. All we could do was sit back for a fortnight and await the outcome of what the doctor said was roughly a 50/50 chance.

These days, when you first dip a toe in the chilling waters of ART and embark on your first cycle, fertility clinics are scrupulous in loading you up with reams of information. There are pamphlets and information sheets on every aspect of the process, from male infertility to health insurance issues, to the counselling services you may need when you discover you would really enjoy slapping the snot out of your doctor. Being a little lost lamb in a strange new world, you conscientiously plough through all the paraphernalia to try to get your head around exactly what you're in for. Forewarned is fore-armed, is it not?

In all of the literature that covers the psychological strain of IVF and similar procedures, there is one constant. Psychologists say that the hardest part of the process, emotionally, is the waiting. I remember scoffing at this when I first read it at the start of our journey. I scoffed, chortled, sneered and jeered myself red-raw. Surely sitting on our arses for two weeks twiddling our thumbs couldn't compare to being poked and prodded, drugged up, cut up and bloated, or looking on virtually helpless as your loved one struggles through it all.

You think the waiting won't be the worst part, and yet, it is. It's a different kind of stress. When you're in and out of hospital, or injecting your loved one, or thrumming up a sperm sample, or slipping in another romantic pessary, at least you're doing something. You, along with your gaggle of doctors and nurses, have at least one hand on the pregnancy tiller. It's unpleasant, time-consuming and more frustrating than playing snooker with your hair on fire, but you tell yourself that every phase you get through could be carrying you toward a positive end result.

After your embryo transfer, all you've got to do for two weeks is to sit. And think. And wonder if that moment just... *now*... on the way to the shops, or at the sink doing the dishes, or collecting the mail is the magical moment when your precious embryos find their home. Or the moment when it's too late and they just fail to be.

In August 2004, Liz and I were both still settling in to part-time work. I was getting regular shifts at the *Courier-Mail* and slowly finding my feet. Ironically, the place was big, a bit impersonal and looked very much like a hospital, so it seemed all too familiar, but there was no orientation for casuals and no easy way to meet people or learn the lie of the land. Like any new cog in a big machine, especially the fast-paced news biz, you are expected to hit the ground running. For my evening shifts on the news desk, all I focused on was slinking into a vacant chair, logging on and getting to it. For a while I felt guilty even getting up for a cuppa. I needed the job and wanted to make a good impression but flying under the radar meant that I had no chance of meeting anyone outside my immediate environment. When I asked who the big guy in the tie was who tended to hang around at night, my new colleagues would look at me strangely before muttering, 'That, Justin, would be the editor.' Apparently they expected a working knowledge of the place to creep into my brain, perhaps by osmosis.

But I kept my eyes and ears open and things slowly improved.

Liz had also fallen on her feet. The stress and odd hours had seen her chuck in the casino experiment, but after filling out a mere 45 forms for only five government departments she managed to gain approval by Queensland's Department of Education to work as a casual primary school teacher. Soon the work began filtering through from various schools in our area, with each workday heralded by a 6.30am phone call. We were both only scoring a day of work here and there, but our living expenses were low, and I was still freelancing from home to help cover our medical expenses.

We were keen to remember what life was like before it was governed by operations and the ingestion of drugs, and what it was like to meet new friends who didn't require samples of our body fluids for keepsakes. We organised outings, we took drives, we kept ourselves busy—anything to fill in periods of unused brain time and keep the whispering doubts at bay.

Sadly, there was not a lot happening in the bedroom at the time. Liz's oestrogen dosage was steadily climbing and she was still on the dreaded progesterone pessaries. Although we never discussed it in so many words, I didn't need her to draw me a diagram. I understood completely. Nothing kills the ardour, it seems, like a constant oily discharge.

A week into our wait and I was actively trying to forget about the deadline looming over us—a sure sign I was struggling.

Pregnancy test? Brain, I don't believe I know what you're talking about. I'm just here, living my life in the now, not thinking about anything, certainly nothing that may or may not be happening in six and three-quarter days from now. Not worrying constantly with my wife about every tiny twinge she feels, every batch of goose-bumps, every transient sensation she can detect, and many she can't. So brain, maybe you need to go and bother someone else. Maybe a few shots of tequila would shut you up, hmmm?

Adding to the building stress was the fact that Liz had noticed a little blood spotting. This might have been the worst of all signs—a precursor to the dreaded period— or a positive sign; a small amount of bleeding caused by the implantation of an embryo into the uterus wall. We were living in abject fear of a tsunami-like period that would clean out her womb, pull down all the IVF ladders we had climbed and send us sliding, kicking and cursing, back down the snake to square one.

So was it good bleeding or bad bleeding? It depended what day you asked. With ten days to go, we had been supremely confident. With five to go, Liz was positive it had all amounted to naught and I'd hit the depths of despair.

We hadn't shared every facet of our IVF saga with our families, but we hadn't held a lot back, and had leant on them often for support. As a consequence, they were all up to date with the state of play embryo-wise, and were strapped into the ride with us. As time ticked away to judgement day, Liz's family were quietly keeping abreast of developments, as was my mum, who was so excited that when she would get talking to strangers in the street most would walk away fully briefed on our progress.

Mum: '...and the egg pick-up went really well, too.'

Man at window: 'That's good news.'

Mum: 'I'll say—they ended up with six healthy embryos.'

Man at window: 'Is that a fact.'

Mum: 'Yes indeed. Not heaps from such good-quality eggs though.'

Man at window: 'Yes, they sound a bit like ours, Madam, the ones on the McMuffin you just ordered. Now please, *please* drive on.'

During this period Liz spend a lot of time discussing our baby-making trials and tribulations with her parents and grandparents, who were only too happy to be in the loop. As far as advice regarding dealing with IVF, as 50-somethings and 80-somethings they naturally had no personal experience to draw from, but they knew that the best thing they could do for Liz was to be her sounding board. They were there from day one of our cycle, as they had been her whole life before that, and this helped her enormously. In her close-knit family, it would have been unusual in the extreme if Liz hadn't sifted through our anxieties, decisions, highs and lows with her family. They had raised her that way, because that is how they help each other cope with life's curve balls.

This is a very healthy and mature way of dealing with life's challenges, but I favour an entirely different method. I call it the 'Stop, Look and Listen' technique. I know many of you guys out there are already using it to some effect, but I'll explain it for the benefit of the others. It works like this: when you confront a major issue or problem in your life, the first step is to STOP thinking about it. Thinking will only allow the problem to occupy your brain for extended periods of time and annoy you. Step two is to LOOK elsewhere for other things to focus your attention on—a hobby or project is always good, or it could be something as simple as work or, ideally, vast amounts of beer. Finally, you must LISTEN to yourself when you really feel, deep down at the core of your being, that you need to drink another six-pack.

When things got tough during our IVF cycle, I would sometimes try to discuss things with my mum or be swept along into discussions with Liz's family, but I found it hard to really open up and would always fall back on the good old Stop, Look and Listen. It didn't actually make me feel any better, but damn, I got a lot of chores done.

Over the next two days our odds improved, more due to what didn't happen rather than anything that did. It was all quiet on the uterine front, which was a sorely needed crumb of good news—no further bleeding, no period, and no indefinable 'bad' feelings seeping through to its owner. The goose had stopped quickstepping across her grave, and I was surprised to discover her outlook was lifting. Balancing that was the natural pessimism that tends to bloom in all of us when we are left without other input. Liz said her boobs weren't sore and, well, she just didn't 'feel' pregnant.

Still, it was possible. Right?

Coincidentally, my mum Jen's first holiday to our new home in Queensland, a trip she had booked months previously, saw her arrive a week before our embryo transfer. Naturally, living in South Australia she had felt isolated from our IVF progress up to this point, so she was revelling in being in the thick of the action at the pointy end of the process. While she didn't want to interfere or contribute to the pressure we were under, in hindsight, living under the same roof with my mother during this time was always going to be challenging, as we were to discover at the most inopportune of junctures.

The first week of Mum's visit was devoted to catching up with Liz's family, sightseeing and op-shopping, and things remained on an even keel for a while, until the dreaded astrology reading. As a surprise, Mum had paid an astrologer friend to do a chart and reading for Liz and me, and she'd recorded her Q and A session with him on tape. Despite not being a true astrology believer, I was happy to take my chart on board, probably because it was quite flattering. Things were going well until part-way into Liz's chart when the astrologer predicted that Liz's first pregnancy would result in a miscarriage.

Given that Mum had been there when the tape was made, I'm sure she would have resorted to a prudent piece of editing had she had her time over again, but she didn't and, as they say, from little things big things grow. That little audio tape was the catalyst for a freeform, multi-faceted, multi-denominational fracas, the likes of which is rarely seen outside a Boxing Day shoe sale.

On pregnancy test eve, I found myself running between my wife (bawling her eyes out in the bedroom) and my mother (sobbing into her red wine downstairs) playing the United Nations peacekeeper and trying to calm everyone down and steer them away from the kitchen knives.

By the time we hit QFG on 2 September for the crucial pregnancy blood test, we didn't know which way was up. Liz was an emotional traffic accident, my mum was hurt but apologetic, and rather than flip-flopping daily, my calculations of our pregnancy odds had begun fluctuating by the minute.

7.54am Thursday 2 September 2004

We've taken a number at QFG for another blood test, physically identical to all the other blood tests Liz has endured over the last year. After once dreading the needle, the blood sliding down the clear tube and the post-test bruising, now she is pretty good at them. She is emotionally wrung out but the nurses keep her talking while they draw off what they need. On this particular Thursday, though, no amount of distraction is going to prevent her churning each possible outcome around in her brain, along with all the baggage from last night.

One glance at the paperwork and the nurse knows it's a pregnancy test, but the only time she acknowledges the gravity of the situation is with a cheery 'good luck' as Liz leaves.

The results will be rushed through and we'll have our yea or nay in one hour.

8.09am Thursday 2 September 2004
What to do for 60 minutes? I can barely think straight, let alone drive, but Liz is much too shaky so I slide into the driver's seat of our semi-new Ford Falcon. We bought it a couple of months back for the dual purposes of carrying my kayak and ... well you need a family car if you're serious about having a family, right? Some may call it wishful thinking; Anthony Robbins would regard it as mentally assuming the attitude of success. Whatever the case, Liz's beloved coupe is gone, and in its place, the Silver Bullet.

I grab the wheel to stop my hands shaking and drive to Fortitude Valley to find a café in which we can kill ... what ... about 50 minutes.

8.59am Thursday 2 September 2004
I know I've eaten breakfast because I just saw it disappear forkful-by-forkful into a gaping hole somewhere under my nose, but I can't tell you if it was eggs or the chicken that laid them. It's something to occupy my hands, as is gulping my complimentary water to calm my racing heart, glancing at my wife and clutching her hand. We

sit on a sunny window seat in an industrial-style James Street café and watch the clock.

The rest of the world is still functioning as normal, if you can believe that. I sit and marvel at all the activity. A series of delivery men push trolleys laden with produce around the nearby stores, power-suited couples stride about with takeaway coffees in one hand and mobiles in the other and through the servery window cooks are sweating and joking over sizzling hotplates.

How can they carry on? Can't they feel the world throbbing and tilting in time with my heartbeat? Don't they know what day it is?

9.08am Thursday 2 September 2004
We're sitting in the car outside the café, and my legs only just got me here. Liz has made the call, and is silently holding her mobile to her ear as I scan her face for clues. After almost two and a half years of failed attempts to get pregnant, today—right now—we get the result of our first IVF cycle.

They can't find the paperwork. Would we mind going on hold?

I feel like we've been on hold since 2002.

The minutes tick by and I listen for a tinny voice from the phone.

God, the cosmic DJ, has his thumb on the LP, slowing down the moment.

Oh God, don't think about God.
Come on! What's the hold-up?

Suddenly it's unbearably hot in the Silver Bullet, and I'm stabbing at a switch but my window won't budge.

'What the fuck is wrong with this friggin'...

I'm on the verge of suffocation when the doc returns and Liz unfreezes her jaw.

'Really? Oh, okay, thanks. Yep, okay. Bye.'

She puts the phone down and looks at me. Twenty-eight months of pain is etched on her face. We burst into tears.

We hug each other in a café carpark and cry a torrent of relief and joy.

THE EGGSHELL SHUFFLE

Everyone needs a hero, so when choosing someone to model your life on, why not shoot for the stars? I try to live my life by the ideals and principles exhibited by one of the twentieth century's finest actors. Whenever I'm faced with a particularly difficult decision or a sticky moral quandary, I ask myself 'What would Daffy Duck do?' You're probably the same.

That's why, when informed that our first cycle of IVF had been successful, my immediate instinct was to find the nearest body of water and bounce head-to-toe across it whooping hysterically.

Far from gravity-defying theatrics, though, when the astounding news came through I was barely able to draw my next breath, suffocating in a car with Liz like a couple of abandoned dogs on a hot day. Despite the lack of oxygen to my brain, however, I knew I'd be all right. The adrenaline in my veins would surely restart my fibrillating heart.

So.

Parents.

Us.

Possibly.

Throughout the previous five months I'd steadfastly maintained to my wife that I knew we were going to get pregnant first go. At times I actually believed myself, and when I didn't I made sure I sang the same tune anyway. Why not? It was equal parts personal affirmation and morale booster for both of us. Now, with a pregnancy confirmed and an embryo-freezing debacle delivering two embryos into Liz's womb, I'd even reignited my twins daydream. Why not again? Before that phone call a double pregnancy had seemed just as far-fetched as a single one, so why couldn't this be twins? Naturally, it was far too early to tell—we'd have to wait for our first ultrasound for that—but seconds after we got the nod I became convinced that we were headed for instant familyhood and started secretly singing a different tune.

Here's the story . . . of a man named Brady . . .

Whether it was one bub or two, as Liz and I sat cooking in our car, tears drying on our cheeks as we struggled to process the information, one phone call had finally dragged us out of the realm of dreams and gut feelings. Now we were dealing with the gold-embossed truth. This wasn't some daydream I'd conjured up that could be laughed off like yesterday's nudie run from the bathroom to the bedroom—it was reality.

The matter-of-factness of Liz's tone on the phone had killed my expectations and I was struggling not to be overwhelmed by the quickfire mood swing. Twenty seconds ago I was dropping with my stomach on the express elevator to despair. Now my head was spinning and I was bursting at the seams to tell someone.

WEHADFUCKINGDONEIT!

No, I wasn't bursting at the seams, I was bursting at the reinforced bits *between* the seams.

We took several gulps of oxygen, grabbed our mobiles and called our mothers, who were both on a breathless standby.

When we told them they also both claimed they'd known all along, the witches, but were nonetheless ecstatic at the news. Liz's due date was 10 May but we quickly warned them off telling anyone outside our immediate family because we both felt like the pregnancy would wink out of existence if Liz sneezed and coughed at the same time, ate a particularly hot curry or caught a glimpse of Daryl Somers on TV. Throughout our treatment the doctors and nurses at QFG were quick to reinforce this thinking and all the IVF literature emphasised the critical initial danger period. Our baby-to-be would not be a bona fide going concern until the twelve-week mark. 'So don't get too excited' was the phrase that hung unsaid off the back of their tales of caution.

The upshot was, at the culmination of two years of medical fandangling, now that all the quit jobs, interstate moves and innumerable lifestyle changes had paid off, we would have to essentially keep our excitement secret for a quarter of a year. While all I wanted to do was bellow it from the rooftops, the brilliant news was to remain a secret until the official press conference just before Christmas. Oh, the cruel irony.

All this talk of danger periods—is there a more apt phrase in this particular context?—got me wondering what the hell was so dangerous about my wife's womb. What are the major perils facing an embryo latched onto a uterine wall? I mean, they made Liz's innards sound like Iraq, swarming with endless hordes of bacterial insurgents fighting good bacteria soldiers like they trot out in those acidophilus commercials. Would our tiny foetuses be caught in the crossfire as the two sides waged a futile and hopelessly misplaced battle for my wife's intestinal health? Had Doctor Smith mistakenly seeded Liz's uterine wall with tiny trip-wires while he was in there delivering the embryos? ('Doctor, you duffer, you've gone and left your probe set on "land mine" again.') But I knew *The Dummy's Guide to Early Pregnancy Pitfalls* was the last tome we needed to crack open at this point, so, in a refreshing change of mid-season form, I shut my mouth and tried to get over it.

My mum had flown home late on the day of the pregnancy test with all of us on speaking terms, which was a minor miracle in itself. Despite the astrologer's prediction, as she left she told us that every spooky motherly instinct she possessed assured her that at least one of our foetuses would successfully storm the beachhead of Liz's uterine shore and win the Twelve-Week War. She was so ready to be a grandma, she said, that the universe had no choice but to make it so. As much as we dismissed out of hand input like this from our family, we needed all the positives we could get to line up against all those drooling, knuckle-scraping what-ifs lurking in the dark.

A couple of weeks into our twelve-week wait, the forces of evil were about to launch a major offensive. My first inkling of this was when I was woken in the wee hours one morning. The bedside light was on, my wife was shaking me and, by the look of horror on her face, a glass of water wasn't going to do it.

She'd had a significant bleed.

'I think it's definitely my period coming on. I've lost an embryo or both or something. Something's not right,' she'd said, barely able to hold back the tears.

'How do you know?'

'Jase, trust me, I know.'

Still groggy, I didn't know which way was up.

It was too much to process. It was a horror movie. It was a knife in the heart and 240 volts in the bowels.

Oh Jesus H. Christ in a motorbike sidecar. 'Well, we'll just see how it goes.' I sat up in bed rubbing my wife's back, staring at the wall and wondering what we would do, how we would function the next day and each day after that.

In the morning, Liz called QFG. We were still terrified, but things always look slightly better in the light of day.

We were under strict instructions to call the nurses if there was any major bleeding, but how major is major?

The nurses asked whether it was bright blood or dark blood. A small amount of dark or old blood could just be the uterus bleeding slightly when the embryos latch on a bit harder, a very normal and very positive sign. Bright or new blood could signal the onset of a period, and we knew what that meant, but how do you judge the difference? We had been told the clinical definitions of bright and dark blood but the voices in our heads were chanting that bleeding couldn't be a good sign. Any slim chance we were clinging to of holding on to the pregnancy had all but evaporated.

In my testosterone-driven quest to nail a set of odds to everything on the planet, I reckoned we'd been boxed in around the bend into the home straight and we'd slumped to 10/1, a mere 10 per cent chance of becoming parents, and twins were right out of the equation. But 10 per cent was still some chance, surely? I tried to convince Liz of this, but only those not attached to the uterus in question still have the luxury of carrying on as if everything is going to be hunky-dory. Liz was still too fragile to start believing in miracles.

She was told to rest and elevate her feet, so she spent most of the next week on the couch, barely daring to let her feet touch the floor. I wasn't sure if this tactic was to stem the bleeding or, as earthy as it sounds, to help keep the embryos in.

Still, the days passed with the train not pulling in at Menstruation Station and our stomachs began to unknot and our breathing deepened. Maybe the little munchkins would hang on after all. We passed the time as we usually did, working, shopping and babytalking to puppies in pet stores. In three years of marriage we had worn many of the sharp edges off each other, and our only real argument at the time was whether Liz was three weeks and three days or three weeks and one day pregnant. (I still maintain to this day that the new pregnancy week started on Monday, not Wednesday, but will she listen?) Liz had the omnipresent oestrogen pills to ingest and innumerable pessaries to insert to help bridge the gap until her body realised it was pregnant and her hormones kicked in, and we paid weekly homage at the temple of Doctor Smith.

We both noticed that Smith had lightened up since we had reinforced his genius by doing the right thing and falling pregnant. In fact, during our visits, he and his secretary gradually nudged their temperature gauges up from icy, past cold and through the stratosphere to tepid. I think I recall seeing his teeth once, but I may have mistaken a smile for his grimace when he slammed a flap of skin in his desk drawer.

The main function of these visits and the subsequent blood tests was for Smith to examine Liz's hormone levels and keep doubling her medication. It got to the point where she was popping oestrogen like Pez and I was buying progesterone pessaries by the kilo.

But time marched on and whatever our man Smith was doing was working.

Six weeks into the pregnancy, it was time for our first ultrasound and we crept into our doctor's rooms barely willing to sit down to hear what news he might deliver.

Technically, twins were still a possibility, but so was nothing at all. We had vaguely discussed the logistics of having twins, and weighed up the usual considerations: the production line of nappies and feeds and heavier financial burden versus the fact that, if we only wanted two kids, maybe we wouldn't have to go through all this again. But it was only a brief conversation. To both of us, discussing the pregnancy felt like it might jinx it. Liz never speculated about twins and I could tell she thought one baby would be more than enough, first time around. I, on the other hand, still harboured secret—and totally unrealistic—dreams of an instant family and a pair of chirpy little tots flashing single-toothed grins from that double-wide pram. I would occasionally find myself humming the accompanying Brady theme song, and casually throwing in a plural when we dared to mention 'the baby' but that was quickly laughed off. It didn't matter. With our day of reckoning approaching, we knew that if one of our little embryos had latched on we would be as over the moon as if two had, just a little less overwhelmed.

It was time.

As Liz moved next door to lie down in his exam room, my pulse was thumping in my ears to the exclusion of all else. The prickly heat that stress brings had me fidgeting like a two-year-old. This ultrasound, more than any other test we'd done, would make or break us. Would there be a foetus there, or even twins, or just an empty space, flushed clean by an unfortunate bleed? I was always the one raising the possibility of twins, but maybe that was just bravado to hide my fear of nothing at all.

To Doctor Smith it was just another day at the office. 'Jason, like to come in to the exam room and have a look?'

'Pardon?' I'd barely realised someone had spoken.

'Er, you'll want to see the ultrasound.'

I did and I prayed my eyes would serve me better than my ears were. I lurched out of my chair and stumbled off after Liz and the doc, into his small adjoining exam room.

We took our places for an unpleasant internal scan. Smith applied the lubricant, then inserted his probe, and a grainy image appeared on the small monitor beside him. The picture bucked, warped and flowed with his movements until he zeroed in on something and we both squinted at the screen, turning our heads like dogs to make out what it was.

It was a tiny, single, precious little baby. Actually, it was a tiny, precious little peanut. Importantly, though, it was a peanut with arm nubs and leg nubs and a heartbeat.

I sat there speechless, grinning in that tiny room like a loon, tearing up and squeezing Liz's hand. Liz kept a lid on her joy, given that she still had a probe up her.

It seemed surreal that we finally had tangible proof of Liz's pregnancy, that Liz—my wife, friend and partner in life—was odds-on to become Liz Davis, wife, friend and *mother* of our child. How could all this IVF heartache really pay off first time? Should we feel guilty? What about all the people who try for *years*? Should we feel the loss of the little embryo that didn't make it?

Ah bugger it. Enjoy the moment, dad-to-be.

That stopped the breath in my pipes. It sounds ridiculous, but we both had been so caught up in the process of getting pregnant that we hadn't really thought about the implications of becoming a parent. Well, we had in the abstract kind of way you do when you plan for what you'll do when you win Lotto, but this was the first step in it *happening*. It was almost as if I hadn't equated pregnancy with being a dad, although the link was starting to hit home very quickly.

On the screen, every now and again our little peanut baby moved and it was all I could do not to cheer. It was better than Friday night football. Peanut's little heart was racing and the blood flow showed up as small strings of colour on the monochrome image. So what if the child's head was as big as the rest of his (or her) body combined. We'd love our little fat-headed Peanut anyway.

We walked out of QFG that morning and ordered our regular celebratory hot chocolates believing, possibly for the first time, that this whole parenthood thing was possible.

While it was generally smooth sailing on the Good Ship Davis, the one pregnancy-based blip on the home radar related to Liz's diet. In her eternal quest to tick every box when it came to protecting the baby, she had read all the do's and don'ts of early pregnancy ever dreamed up, many related to diet. This 'helpful' information came from pregnancy books, QFG info sheets and the general mass media and, if women believed it all, they would be reduced to a diet of organically grown, triple-washed carrots with a bran flake enema for afters, but only when filtered through the flaxen hair of an Icelandic virgin.

I have compiled the following list of foods that various sectors of the community believe are dangerous to consume during pregnancy: rare beef, lamb and pork, all undercooked poultry, seafood, alcohol, tea, coffee, chocolate, all soft cheeses including fetta, pate, raw egg, any pre-prepared salad, salad dressing (unless prepared before your eyes), any form of leftovers and all food even loosely associated with a salad bar or bain-marie. This is *on top* of any allergies or dietary requirements you may already have.

As you can imagine, sticking to this regimen will put a severe dent in your diet, and Liz's constant worrying, wondering and second-guessing quickly got on my nerves. Selfishly, I was thinking more about the annoyance I suffered when we were forced to conduct a Royal Commission when ordering from a menu than what must have been a crushing sense of obligation for Liz every time she conspired to consume. I reasoned that surely some of this advice was taking nutritional safety to the nth degree, and the chances of contracting listeriosis or any other disease named after a Greek holiday resort was microscopically low.

It took me many weeks to realise that Liz probably agreed with me, but was in an impossible position. The what-ifs were back and they were crushing her: what if that delicious tuna steak, pink and luscious in the middle and perfectly cooked, contained some microscopic nasty that was later found to have damaged our unborn baby? What if she beat my brains in with the heel of her shoe if I rolled my eyes one more time at her menu indecisiveness?

Our other arguments were less intense and tended to ebb and flow as the weeks passed. Pretty soon we were having the 'are we twelve weeks or is this the twelfth week' discussion, which could mean only one thing...

We had (gulp) made it to our twelve-week scan, in the process graduating from doctor ultrasounds to a proper, mainstream clinic. Having your IVF doctor scan your tiny foetus in his cramped exam room is one thing, but stepping out of the shadows and into the more public river of medical normalcy felt to me like a huge leap. This was a chic ultrasound clinic in the real world. It was cool and quiet, with couples, pregnant women and families whispering to each other in the reception area and trying to focus on the magazines at hand. Periodically women would pad across the carpet and disappear down a corridor with their better halves or leave grandma and grandpa to try various sleeper holds on little Billy while they checked on his sibling-to-be.

We waited our turn and were eventually ushered into a darkened consulting room dominated by an exam bed, a floor-standing computer/ultrasound contraption and a big monitor on top of a cupboard.

Our technician was a stoic-looking man who shook my hand and made an effort to smile as Liz got up on the bed and I took my seat. Soon the goo was applied and the familiar grainy picture distorted, disappeared and then materialised. And there he or she was, much larger than last time and with a comical case of the hiccups that caused his/her whole body to leap a few millimetres in the air.

While we were grinning like lobotomy patients in piles of their own poo, for some reason our technician was replaced by a smiley woman, but we weren't to be distracted. She busied herself dragging a cursor across the screen and drawing dotted lines to take measurements of the foetus. Occasionally she would press a button and a still image for us to take home would ooze out of the machine. The initial structure of a face was visible in the photos, the tiny human even managing to shove a thumb in the hole below its two bud-like bulbous eyes and button nose. The machine spat out some 3-D renderings of the scans, a whiz-bang option that fudged the flat images into 3-D shapes that alternately delighted us and frightened us into silence. In some we could see something resembling the face of our little baby, in others its features had been strangely distorted and combined with the contours of surrounding tissue, a bit like Jeff Goldblum at the end of *The Fly*. Needless to say, those ones won't be making it into the album. We paid extra, though, for a video version of the ultrasound session— just a silent twenty-minute record of the hiccupping baby and measuring cursor flitting around the screen drawing lines along its limbs. I think my mum played it until the tape wore out.

The technician measured everything a few times with special emphasis on the thickness of a membrane behind the little tyke's neck. This measurement is called the nuchal translucency and determines the likelihood of your baby having Down syndrome, she explained.

The smile fell from my face. Down syndrome? I craned forward to make out the minuscule figures on the side of the screen. Did it say 1.4mm? Then, after a few beats of silence, I asked a question that she had probably heard slightly less than 20,000 times during her career.

'So what's a good score?'

Her well-rehearsed response—that there is no 'good' and 'bad' scores, just different probabilities, and these weren't ironclad either—did little to satisfy. It is just an indicator that could lead to further tests.

Yeah, yeah, I get it, but what does it look like to you?

I squinted up at the screen again. Peanut did look a little chubby behind the neck region. Maybe that was where he stored his fat for winter. Oh God.

After Liz was de-gooped and on her feet, we followed our technician into a small interview room and went through the results. As she started out on her technical spiel I was miles away, staring at the tabletop onto which laminated images of Down syndrome foetuses were stuck. Those unfortunate kids had some big neck membranes, much thicker than our little Peanut's. I relaxed further when she said Peanut's individual risk factor of Down's was about 1 in 3500.

'But remember,' she added, 'the reason there's a one in the equation is that it's always possible.'

Our ultrasound pics took pride of place on the fridge and my mum loved the video, but the technician had left us with a gift that no amount of money can buy: something else to worry ourselves sick over.

Finally, the time had come to spill our guts, and shout our good news from the nearest rooftop. In an inexplicable (or actually very splicable, when I thought about it) turn of events, it seemed the news had leaked out to several non-family-members, all of whom were friends of Liz's. Since I hadn't told anyone, and they had no other way of finding out, it was clear what had happened—advanced computer viruses had harvested the information from our brains as we slept and broadcast it to the general populace. Obviously.

So I had to get in quickly before Deep Throat told all my friends too. I called Derek in the UK, who knew exactly why I was calling out of the blue, and then worked my way down my list of mates. Everyone was extremely happy for us, especially those who knew we'd been through IVF, but no-one's reaction quite matched my expectations. I was so happy I was in danger of bursting a blood vessel. I was happier than was recommended by the surgeon-general but, looking back, it's impossible for friends or family to be as thrilled as a parent-to-be, and it has to be that way. If the parents aren't at the top of the excitement tree, they've probably got a problem.

So, we went from officially 'having trouble' to officially up the duff, in only 23,967 easy steps.

This is not to say that we considered ourselves home and hosed. Far from it. In our house we couldn't even say the words 'pregnant' or 'baby' without following it with a wood-touching qualifier. The sky above was still constantly threatening to slip off its skyhooks and crash into our craniums, but even stress monkeys like us are forced to admit when things are going well. And after only a month of constant affirmations we usually believed it.

A couple of weeks before the twelve-week ultrasound Liz had been allowed to finally start tapering off her medication. For her not to be constantly shoehorning drugs into every orifice was a big relief to both of us, and by the time we were scheduled to see our new (*gasp! cheer!*) obstetrician, she had only a day or two to go before she was completely natural, pedalling on her own without the training wheels. The IVF process had been brilliant in terms of our positive result (touch wood) but we were keen to leave it on the roadside behind us and carry on lost in the anonymity of an ordinary pregnancy. Callous as it is, the individual attention and resources allocated to you during ART treatment are critical until the instant you get what you want. After that point you just want to be left alone to be pregnant like everyone else.

In the spirit of shedding the accoutrements of IVF, we'd opted not to use the obstetric services of Doctor Smith. We were grateful for the calculated, results-driven treatment we'd received from him, but it was time to move on.

Liz's GP and the nurses at QFG had recommended an obstetrician called Bob Watson who, from all accounts, was a caring doctor with a compassionate bedside manner. So, in October 2004, we steeled ourselves for the culture shock and took our first trip out to North West Private Hospital. I also secretly set myself the task of saying something clever in his rooms and following it up with, 'Why, it's elementary, my dear Watson' (head waggle optional). A super-witty rejoinder never goes astray as an icebreaker and I envisioned him exploding with laughter, clapping us both on the back and offering to deliver our baby (touch wood) for free. I really need to get a hobby.

Watson was a tall, dark-haired, friendly fellow who seemed to be somehow butler-like, quick to offer a hearty handshake, always standing at the door to his rooms bent forward slightly at the waist, welcoming us in. We liked him immediately. He reminded me of someone and I could never quite figure out who it was until I asked Liz later and she uttered the words 'George Jetson'. Yes, meet a dark-haired George Jetson (dum dum DA dum), ready to deliver the babies of the twenty-first century.

Liz hadn't suffered much from morning sickness, the main noticeable symptom being a sudden aversion to tea in the morning due to a constant bad taste in her mouth. She became very particular about what she would eat and craved healthy food in general. Other than that, there were occasional lightning waves of nausea, but they came and went before they really made their presence felt. She was free of synthetic hormone assistance and was feeling surprisingly well.

During our first visit Doctor Watson gave Liz a clean bill of health. Everything was within normal limits and looking good. To my delight he decided to do another ultrasound, and we got another look at our little son-or-daughter, still doing well in there (touch wood) and still with the heart rate of an Olympic sprinter. I looked over Bob's shoulder at the screen and was soon grinning and babytalking at the monitor again.

The visit had gone swimmingly—the difference between Smith and Watson was like the gulf between Coke and cordial. The only thing that had been missing was the chance to set up the conversation to deliver my hilarious Watson line.

At this point there was no way to tell if the baby was a boy or a girl. The little penis I thought I'd fleetingly glimpsed on the ultrasound was imaginary, a product of my not-so-secret desire for a son and heir to continue my important work in assembling the largest horror movie collection in my street. Liz, predictably, was keen for a girl. We're not ones to mess with the natural order of things.

The baby clothes had already started arriving from both of our mums, small amounts at first to test the waters, then in greater numbers, but they were all still unisex and colour-neutral, blue and pink noticeably absent. Liz's mum Sue was excited but my mum was beside herself. In a room with Tim Shaw and the late Big Kev, I'd back my mum to be leading the conga line.

She had recruited her entire church to pray for the safe arrival of our unborn baby and little packages kept arriving, filled with tiny singlets, booties and jumpsuits. She would be quite possibly the proudest grandmother in the world, and the smart money was on her moving north to Queensland to be on hand well before the baby was on its feet. I gave her six months before the pull of secondary motherhood proved too strong.

With the safe arrival of our child becoming more likely with every passing day (touch wood), there were certain issues that now had to be addressed. Chief among these was the unsightly lump in the corner of what would now be the baby's room. Yes, my study would be reverting back to its former title of The Third Bedroom for the sole tenuous reason that the baby should have its own room. Not born yet and running the show. So, in November 2004, at a meeting of the joint chiefs of staff of our house, it was decided that I, who needed his own work space from which to generate income for the family, would be banished from upstairs and sent to work in purgatory, under the house. I was in favour of a bilateral shared approach to the room, in which I would continue to annex 10 per cent of the territory for my desk in exchange for certain trade concessions (i.e. I would agree to finance the child until roughly the age of 25, and he or she would agree to let me). But I was outvoted when the most powerful faction in the upper house (Liz) created a voting bloc by forming a coalition with the second-most powerful faction (the dogs). And lo, it was decided.

I would build my own study under our house and move in before the new tenant for the third bedroom took up the lease.

In our house, being a raised weatherboard Queenslander, this was perfectly feasible. By December I'd plucked an ad out of the local rag and employed a team of rough-looking but surprisingly competent concreters to take up a section of the sloping concrete floor and lay a flat room-sized slab in its place. They did their part admirably, and the renovating baton was once again passed to me. I had about five months to build some wall frames, put in some windows and hang a door. How hard could that be?

Two weeks before Christmas, again not quite believing we'd made it that far, we trotted back to the chic ultrasound clinic for the twenty-week scan (to be taken in Liz's nineteenth week). Liz's mum and dad were visiting from Sydney at the time, and Liz's mum, Sue, came with us to the clinic on the way to a spot of maternity-wear shopping and ended up joining us for the scan.

This time, our ultrasound technician was a nice young woman with a soothing voice and an English accent and she soon had Liz horizontal with goo on her belly and set about massaging it in with her ultrasound wand.

Liz had been under strict instructions to drink two large glasses of water an hour before the test, presumably to make the ultrasound waves conduct better through her organs, but this just meant she was busting to pee by the time we were ushered into our scan room.

She strained and clenched to hold on through the first part of the scan, but when the operator saw how squashed her giant bladder had made the baby, she gave Liz permission to go off and ease the pressure. When she returned, our recalcitrant baby had more room to play with, but wouldn't sit still long enough for the technician to do all the required measurements and checks. We had to sit and wait until it took a break from its exercise video before we could take care of business.

In the previous seven weeks the baby had really put on a lot of size and this had added greatly to its personality. Now it really looked like a little human being, and exhibited some of the same traits as kids outside the womb (apart from that glue-eating fetish, which was big when I was a lad).

He or she was sucking his/her thumb, and even entertained us with another comical bout of hiccups, general capering and some random arm movements that we took to be waves. I was surprised by how advanced the formation of the baby's face was and the little details we could make out, like the child's individual fingers and toes, and the slightly creepy glimpses inside its body to check its brain and other organs. We even watched as the baby's four heart valves worked through their cycle. First a toothbrush with a flexible head, and now *this*.

Eventually I got the courage to raise a question that had been plaguing me: can you determine the sex at this point? I'd been straining for a glimpse of a penis— or the space where one should have been—without much luck. With the baby side-on and oodles of umbilical cord in the way, it was difficult to tell. Liz and I had already come to an understanding that she didn't want to know what sex our child was, but I'm not one for surprises. The last thing I wanted to have happen at the birth was a shadow of disappointment flash across my face when the doctor held up my new daughter. I was 99 per cent sure this wouldn't happen, that I'd be thrilled with anything the doc handed me, but I figured it might be useful for me to be comfortable with the idea prior to that point. So I asked if the technician would tell me the sex and not tell Liz. Surprisingly, she said no problem and after a few more measurements and take-home pics were reeled off, she asked me outside and whispered in my ear, 'I think it's a girl.' She said the baby was in a difficult position to be able to tell, but that was what she was betting on.

Then I realised it was a notion that sat well with me. I walked back in to collect Liz and Sue with a huge grin on my face, and they immediately assumed our baby would have tackle, but vowed to not ask and wait to be surprised at the birth.

They held out a full half-hour.

I was no help, of course. I was like the cat that swallowed the canary-flavoured mouse, indulging in advanced forms of mind games such as skipping up the street chanting 'I know something you don't know', and tittering like an imbecile.

Before our obligatory post-consultation coffee shop stop, the womenfolk ducked into a maternity shop, where Liz began trying on swimmers. The matronly owner of the shop started with all the usual chitchat about due dates and feeling well, then asked what sex it was. I kept my mouth shut and asked her to tell me. She took a quick look at Liz and almost immediately picked it as a girl. 'You can tell because she's lying wrapped around horizontally. Boys tend to sit straight out in front more.'

During our non-coffee drinks break, Liz finally caved and begged to know, so I confessed that the Maternity Shop Witch had been right. The witch later told me that she had a 94 per cent strike rate.

Cue *Twilight Zone* theme.

During the last month of 2004, the pregnancy and our moods in general just kept getting better. Liz and I were getting along well, even though we were still tiptoeing on eggshells for fear of jinxing the baby, our trepidation was dropping steadily and we were getting used to the idea that, hey, maybe everything would be all right. Why shouldn't it work for us? We deserved that much, right?

We started to allow ourselves to get just marginally excited.

During our Christmas shopping expeditions we began gravitating towards previously unexplored regions of major department stores, and we would snap out of dreamland while running the soft fabric of a baby bonnet through our fingers or sending a colourful mobile twirling above a cot. I suddenly became extremely interested in baby stroller engineering, and would conduct impromptu shock absorber testing on the more expensive models.

'Oooh, Liz, dual wishbone suspension and anti-lock brakes.'

'Get out of that thing, you idiot. You'll break it.'

I had even started to pick up on the season's cool characters and toddler fashions. I learned there'd been a changing of the guard in kiddy character-related merchandise. Ballerina Mouse had long ago left her little ballerina droppings all over the Bratz dolls and yet Pooh and Tigger were still keepin' it real for the Sesame Street set. I suddenly found toys with pullstring-activated soundtracks cute, rather than suppressing a burning desire to drop-kick them into the next postcode, and I took an unhealthy interest in breast pump technology.

Occasionally, in the middle of dinner, or while walking the dogs, Liz would turn to me out of the blue and whisper, 'Holy crap, Jase. There's a baby inside of me' or 'What if we become parents?' I shared the same incredulity, but I could tell Liz's expression was tinged with a metallic vein of fear.

She, more than I, bore the responsibility of ensuring the safe gestation of our baby and such a responsibility can do little but weigh heavily. Every foodstuff was a potential hazard, every chemical or cleaning product a possible sinister influence on our unborn child. Yes, everything was going well, but what if one stupid mistake undid all our luck and hard work? All that pain and angst would have been for nothing.

Liz struggled to stay positive and sometimes teetered on the brink of obsession. She had little choice. What if she tripped over and felt a twinge? What if she walked through a cloud of secondhand smoke, undercooked the chicken or forgot her vitamins? Would that be enough to damage our fragile foetus? In looking at the mountain we'd scaled on our journey so far, she couldn't help but see how far we had to fall.

So on she went, double and triple-checking what went onto her plate, sticking to her restrictive diet and popping her vitamins with military precision. She was doing everything in her power to bring a healthy baby safely into the world, and I was thankful for the sacrifices she was making.

For me though, the future held almost no fear now. I knew the risks but somehow I also knew our baby would be healthy and I knew we'd make brilliant parents. Everything was going to be okay.

THE REVOLVING DOOR

Liz was waiting with the phone in hand when I drove in under the deck. Her face was pale, with a tight expression that told me it was not the Lotto people asking when they could back up the money truck. The faces of possible callers, ones that could be the bearers of bad news and would want to talk to me, flashed through my brain. One minute I was popping down to the service station for some mower fuel, ready for a sunny morning of turf maintenance, the next it looked like I should be bracing myself. But for what?

'It's Kevin.'

'Kevin?'

'That guy who's boarding with your mum.'

Mum had told me about a 50-something local bloke she had helped get into a community housing unit in her home town. They had developed a good friendship over a couple of years and when he was having trouble with bikie neighbours at his new place she offered to let him stay with her until the fiends next door were given the flick. I gathered that the deal was more about companionship than cash, and I'm not sure if he actually paid her anything or just helped around the house. As a 54-year-old woman living alone, Mum had found it handy to have a man around the place, but not in *that* way. She had said the arrangement was entirely platonic and that it had been working out well for about three months. Excellent.

But Kevin on the phone meant Mum.

I'd only spoken to Kevin once or twice before but it was clear that this time he was distressed. I don't remember the details of the conversation, only the overall gist. 'I've got some bad news…'

Understatement-wise, they don't get much bigger.

Among the torrent of words punctuated by agonised deep breaths, I eventually pieced it together. The previous night Mum had collapsed from something that might have been a heart attack or a brain haemorrhage, he wasn't sure, but he tried to administer CPR and she wasn't responsive and he called an ambulance and then the ambos tried to revive her and they took her to the hospital but they don't have intensive care so a chopper was called and she was flown up to Flinders Medical Centre in Adelaide.

While Kevin unloaded his news, I was still dredging what Mum had told me about him from my mental microfiche, and so to process what he was telling me took some doing. I tried to stop my head spinning by quickly thwapping on my journalist's hat. *What else do I need to know about the when, why and how of this situation? Where do I go from here?*

Kevin did his best to provide a few details, but he sounded as addled as I felt. He'd been in the thick of the tragedy long enough for the emotion to swamp him, while I was still in a cottony cocoon of shock. Kevin gave me the number of a doctor at the Flinders Medical Centre Critical Care Unit, and I was to ring without delay.

First I had to concentrate long enough to relay some of the facts to Liz. The most crucial of these—Mum's condition—was the most elusive. Since Kevin wasn't family, he hadn't been given any updates since the previous night, when the ambulance had taken Mum away. But performing CPR on an unresponsive patient is a very bleak starting point.

I rang the doctor. I can't remember his name, but he sounded young and caring, but not beyond cutting straight to the medical chase. It must come with the territory. He told me some things I already knew and a few shocking truths that I didn't. My mother had indeed collapsed the previous night in her house and, after sustained CPR, had been airlifted to the Critical Care Unit of Adelaide's biggest hospital.

Oh Christ. This is real.

Although the ambulance officers had continued CPR when they arrived, the length of the time lapse between her collapse and the start of the resuscitation by Kevin was unclear. This was important in determining any secondary damage to the brain.

Pacing up and down our back deck oblivious to the glorious sunshine, I remember wishing that the doctor's calm, measured monologue would both speed up and stop altogether. I was struggling to stop my voice cracking and my vision was swimming with tears.

'We've run a series of tests and we believe a large brain aneurysm—that's a burst blood vessel in the brain— caused her collapse. I'm sorry to say that she is unresponsive and on a ventilator...'

Somewhere, a doctor was still speaking...

'Appears to be quite a lot of damage...'

'...series of tests. They need to be replicated by another doctor...'

Butsheismymum...she'llbeokay...mymumwillbeokay...

'If you can come down...'

'... I would understand if you didn't want to. It's personal choice...'

It was like trying to get back onto a speeding conveyer belt. I had to get my mental legs pumping before I could rejoin the conversation.

'But do you expect her to recover?'

'I'm afraid that's very unlikely. There has probably been two lots of damage to your mum's brain—what looks to be extensive damage from the aneurysm and possibly other damage from the oxygen deprivation after that.'

The next ugly question sat there in front of me, daring me to ask it. Could we really be this far down the road

already? 'If she doesn't recover... do I have to say when...
is there a point at which the machines get turned off?'

'Let me assure you, you don't have to make any
decision like that. It's an automatic procedure that begins
if and when another doctor examines her and gets the
same results I did. If again there is found to be nil brain
activity, then she is pronounced brain dead. There is no
decision you have to make.'

Brain dead.

'Brain dead. So there's no chance she'll recover...'

Brain dead.

'Actually, I'm very sorry to say that in this situation
it would probably be better that she didn't.'

It was Monday 27 December 2004.

After the phone call, I find the next realistically gettable
flight to Adelaide, Liz helps me pack a bag and we shove
off for the airport. The most constructive thing she can
do for me, I tell her, is to stay at home and look after
our unborn baby. This is true enough, and with dogs
and the house to look after it is easier for her to stay,
but the subtext (which I'm sure is writ large across my
face) is that if there's the slightest chance of the stress
of the situation affecting her, well... on top of this, if
anything happens to her or that baby inside her it will
probably kill me.

So three hours after filling my two-stroke can I'm on
a plane and three hours after that I'm stepping off it
and into another long, desiccated Adelaide summer
evening. If there was anyone sitting next to me during

the three-hour flight to Adelaide I didn't notice them. How could I? I hardly looked up from my book. I was getting through only a sentence or two every few minutes, but reading those sentences to within an inch of their lives. At the end of each one I could not remember how it began.

Kevin had promised to meet me at the airport and Liz had called him with the flight details. Over the years I have made that windy walk across the tarmac to the terminal many times, my mum radar on high alert to pick out the little figure in the crowd with the big grin and the tear in her eye. As the years passed and she shrank in comparison, I had to bend further to catch the surprisingly strong hug that was wound up in her, but it was always there.

Now, as I tromp into the throng of greetings, waves and excited kids holding balloons, I'm still half-expecting to see her, squeezing between the tall people to intercept me, or standing to the side out of harm's way.

But no. Instead I wander around away from the luggage crush looking for a man with an English accent. I have never met him and wouldn't go out of my way to know him if not for the circumstances, which he has absorbed and is somehow now tainted by. The bad-news man.

Of course this is grossly unfair, and the way he told it he had done his best to help Mum after he found her, so I steel myself to be polite. If he hadn't been there she might have stayed there for days.

Do NOT think about that...

I see a man of about the right age in a strange bucolic get-up. He looks lost and red-eyed and is clutching a hanky, so I'm pretty sure it's him. A couple of pleasantries and the accent seal the deal. It's hard to know what to say, and he looks permanently close to tears. We look at each other and are about to strike out for the carpark when he grabs me in a spontaneous hug. Even more awkward. The whole situation is just dripping with shit.

The only thing I can do is keep going. We get to the car and I am slightly taken aback to find it is Red Fred, Mum's car, but then logic kicks in and I reason that, hey, the guy has no other easy way to get here, so I suck it up and brace for what comes next.

Kevin is barely holding it together, to the point where I am worried that he shouldn't be driving, but we make it to the sprawling hospital complex and he leads me through the warren of jumbo lifts, anonymous white halls and acronym-heavy signage. The place looks deserted and slightly scuffed, like it's just waiting to discharge its last lot of patients before being renovated or demolished. At the end of the warren we find the Critical Care Unit.

A friendly grey-haired woman is propped at a bare desk, reading a romance novel and guarding the entrance. A small plaque reveals her name, and that she is a volunteer. When I tell her who I am, she heads up a hallway, punches a code into a keypad and disappears through a glass security door. An eternity later a wavy-haired doctor emerges and ushers me into an interview room so blankly utilitarian as to wipe your memory of

it before you even leave. Its only unusual features are
the fresh boxes of tissues scattered around.

Inside, the doctor I spoke to earlier (Stewart?) perches
himself on the edge of a worn chair, lowers his voice
and is very sorry to tell me many things. The first is that
my mum is unaware of the outside world. A blood vessel
in her brain has burst, causing massive damage, and there
is no realistic hope of any form of recovery. All the tests
that have been done have confirmed that my once cheery,
cheeky, loving mother is now an empty shell.

'The term we use is brain death, or nil brain function,'
he tells me again.

He is soon talking to another empty shell. *Seven hours
ago I had a mum; I was part of a family. I could count
on a phone call after 6pm every week or so with all her
news. I'd known all the bit-players in the bulletin and
they'd known of me. Now there's no-one. Of course I
have Liz, and my in-laws and family overseas and a few
long-lost people scattered around, but why do I feel like
I'm fifteen and getting the 'sorry, son, you are now an
orphan' speech?*

No. NOPE. Nuh-uh. This doesn't happen. You can't just
call someone, pull them out of the real world and pull
this stunt. Mum is sick, maybe, but she is still there, and
just on the other side of the security door, right? The
doctor is addressing the situation like . . . a situation, not
the flesh-and-blood person who raised me and subsequently
invented 'face dancing', a revolutionary, boredom-killing
musical gurning concept so stupid and hilarious that it
can only be performed to audiences wearing absorbent

undergarments. But the doctor's analytical approach is good in a crazy kind of way. Something in me is desperate to hang on to this detached point of view. That way I can avoid dealing with the emotional tsunami building off the coast, and as soon as they tell me it has all been a mistake—that Doctor Barry had a fight with his wife that morning and forgot to turn the pesky cranial spectramometer *on* before taking the reading—it will be a shorter path back to normalcy.

The first cracks appear when the doctor throws in, as an aside, that one of the tests doctors perform to check for primitive reflex reactions and therefore brain function is putting their finger on a naked eyeball.

My mum, lying there, with a finger on her open eye.

'So the blink reflex is a pretty basic one, and there was no movement...'

'Okay, can I go in and see her?'

'Of course.'

Outside the room I find Kevin dabbing at his raw eyes and working at his nose with a sodden hanky. It's time to go in, and a nurse takes us through the security door and we are told to head to the wash station to wash our hands with an evaporating alcohol solution. Then we squeak across the lino, turn a corner and the CCU opens up before us.

The place is deathly quiet, with only the sporadic muted beeping of monitors to break the air-conditioning hum. If a doctor or nurse speaks, it is in hushed tones, as if the collective grip on life in here is so fragile a shout could kill.

There are twenty or so beds in the huge room, each in its own bay and most with green privacy curtains drawn. Those that are open are home to various motionless human beings plugged in to the machines that surround them. Few eyes are open, breathing is slow and mechanical—they are all obviously in dire straits.

The bays are arranged in two rows with a square nurses' station on a raised platform between them. On it nurses and doctors fuss over charts and man the phones as we are led to a point midway along the far row. Kevin knows enough to walk behind me.

We stop and I can barely look in.

There she is.

Tiny. Tucked in. Pale. Vacant.

Mouth agog around the tubes bisecting her lips.

Kevin sits down and I listen to the regular hiss and wheeze of the ventilator and watch the black breathing bellows rise and fall in its plastic chamber.

Mercifully, her eyes are closed, but I sense they are about to flutter open, which will startle us all, and then we'll rally around and help her with her recovery or rehabilitation or whatever she needs. One day we'll even shock ourselves with our first laugh about the situation.

But her eyes stay shut. They have that fresh, relaxed look of someone enjoying an afternoon catnap, but the tube in her mouth draws my attention too easily and forces me to realise that my hope is a daydream.

I step up to the bed, pluck her hand up and rub it between mine. It is surprisingly warm and soft, but a dead weight.

Dead.

The tears start to flow and they won't stop. So I finally let go and let them go. I stand there, legs locked against weak knees, rubbing her hand and weeping like a toddler with a skinned elbow.

There is nothing else. I start to lapse into a stringy-salivaed chant. *'Ohmumohmumohmum...'*

Kevin's hug from behind snaps me out of it and I sit down, drawing my spit back where it should be. I can't look at him, so I look at the floor.

Kevin has brought her hairbrush and he steps forward and begins to tug at her hair with it, trying to fashion it into a style from its wild arrangement around her head. It is killing me, him tugging and fussing and dripping tears onto her bedsheets. He sobs quietly, but his tears dry mine up and replace them with anger. Upon reflection, I suppose I am just mad at the situation and the world and the hospital for allowing this to happen, but he is wearing the blame.

After an hour or two or twenty minutes by her bedside, I am spent and need to go away and regroup. Kevin says he'll stay, presumably to finish his hairdressing appren-ticeship.

I walk back outside to the waiting area shaking my head—it is like he is running the show here. One of the staff had even done a double take when I informed him that he wasn't my mum's partner. Okay, he'd known her two or three years, but his constant grief-stricken reminis-cences are trampling my years of memories. I am having enough trouble coping with this. I can't be a crutch for him to use to get him through in *his* hour of need.

It is getting late and eventually Kevin comes out and we make a rendezvous time to meet back here in the morning. He drives me around to a taxi rank in another part of the hospital (he's driving Red Fred like an old hand and I'm feeling the kind of strong male instinct that nearly makes me jump out despite the fact we're doing 50km/h) and I disappear post-haste into the back of a cab.

Across on the other side of the city, I lobbed on my friend Bart's doorstep, wrung out to a husk and in need of a few lighter moments to balance out my head. As one of my oldest friends, and a bona fide oddbod like myself, he was eminently qualified. Bart is the kind of friend that, upon receiving a call out of the blue from a bloke he hasn't seen in a year asking if he can crash at his place that night, only asks, 'What flavour pizza?'

After I relayed the Mum news to Bart and he gathered his jaw up off the floor, thoughts turned to beer, and scads of it. Of course, he expressed shock, incredulity and sorrow at my and my mum's situations, but he instinctively knew where to draw the line. It may sound callous, but all I wanted from the evening was a few beers, a laugh or two if we could manage it and some conversation that didn't involve blood vessels going pop in the night. I already knew how fucked the situation was—mercifully Bart didn't spend the evening reminding me.

Instead, we did the obligatory gourmet pizza and movie run. Having been on the clean-living wagon (I can reveal that it's a horse-drawn Amish affair) for the best part of three years, this was a treat. In the video store, Bart indulged me and hired *Dawn of the Dead* and we spent the best part of an evening chatting and drinking beer and yelping with fright and laughter as the undead swarmed across the Earth, terrorising a small band of survivors. I have mulled over why I have always loved horror movies so much, and the reason is this: it may sound strange, but as crappy as your day may have been or as insurmountable as your problems may appear, this will always seem trivial when faced with (for example) a lone fight against a planet full of ravenous, flesh-eating sub-humans. The next time you're feeling down, try it. You'll see it's true. I walked out of *The Ring* like it was Christmas Day.

But the light mood couldn't last. The next day I was back at the hospital by 9am knee-deep in my own personal horror movie.

There was no news. Mum was in the same bay in the same bed in the same position. The only thing that had changed was the nurse who took me in to see her. A night's sleep and another long drive up from Victor Harbor had not improved Kevin's state of mind either. He was still incredibly upset, and felt the need to tell me so at every opportunity. I was cracking badly but I had to maintain some sort of grip. Should she not... improve, I was solely responsible for what happened to her next; to her life, her dignity, her body, animals and possessions. But the pressure was starting to mount and all the extra weight was sinking me into a quicksand of anguish from which I could barely function. The only way to get by was to focus on what needed to be done.

I met with a more senior CCU doctor about Mum's condition and, unlike his junior colleague, this medico had obviously been around the unit so long he was hardened to the tragedy that ebbed and flowed through the place. We sat in the same interview room as the day before and he delivered the 'I'm sorry' speech from memory but it didn't hit his eyes.

Overnight checks had confirmed the first doctor's grim diagnosis and it seemed staff were only waiting on another doctor to formally replicate those results and then wheels would begin to turn. 'For patients in a confirmed state of brain death, like your mum, the procedure is then automatic,' he said.

In 24 hours things had become automatic, cut-and-dried, mechanical. I stared down at a mark on the man's shoe. 'I know she looks like she is just going to wake up,' he said, 'but let me assure you there is absolutely no chance of that happening.' They don't take the next step lightly, he said. They had exhausted every check known and come up empty. Then he said the word 'harvest' and the word 'organs' and something about the coroner investigating to confirm the cause of death. I had already slipped over into numbness.

Mum and I had discussed organ donation in passing over the years and she was all for it. She had ticked the organ donor box on her licence renewal and had checked that I had as well, so I knew where she stood. Add to that the fact that she was an active community worker and lived to help others, and there was no doubt in my mind of her wishes. When I told the doc this, I could tell he was pleased, but didn't want to show it.

I only had one question. 'Will I be told when it's my last chance to say goodbye? I don't want to miss it.'

'Yes, of course. You won't miss it.'

Next, another meeting, this time with a nice woman called Kathy from the South Australian Organ Donation Agency. We filled out forms and went through the same questions again.

It was a wonderful thing we were doing. We could help up to ten people. She drank and smoked? It didn't necessarily matter. What about her eyes, her liver, her lungs? The coroner's office needed to confirm a cause of death, so they would have to remove her brain to examine for an aneurysm after her organs were harvested for donation. What did I want done with her brain?

Soon it was done, the die was cast and Mum would be helping people as she had all her life. But why did she have to be 'harvested' to do it?

I needed a breather, but what I got was a large dose of Kevin and me sitting in a coffee shop in an adjoining building divvying up the list of bad news phone calls. With scads of telephone change in hand, I got to relive the whole delightful experience over and over. And over.

One of the calls I made was to Dave and Helen, a married couple Mum and my dad had known since their hippy adventures in the 60s. My father and Dave had served in the Navy together, and after Mum and my dad split up when I was two, Dave and Helen remained friends of hers. They were relaxed folk and I enjoyed their company and lapped up their stories of my mum, dad and me as a baby in the freewheeling 70s. Since my dad left us when I was so young and died in 1996 with almost no contact over the years, they were one of my few links with that part of my heritage.

Like everyone I would call that day, Dave and Helen were shocked and horrified but, true to form, they dropped everything and promised to meet me at the hospital in a couple of hours. Finally some allies from the old days to help me get by. I felt my load get a few kilos lighter, but that may have been the dollar coins I was offloading into the hospital payphone.

When Kevin and I met Dave and Helen at the CCU the place was in chaos. It was standing room only in the waiting area, with a huge group of family and friends clutching each other and wailing at the awful shock of whatever had happened to whoever had just arrived. If I thought it was a desperately unhappy place before, now it was hell on earth. I eventually pieced together that there was a young guy inside who had made a tremendous mess of himself on a motorbike, and we passed the time looking on as his distressed relatives came and went. The sobbing and wailing bounced off the walls, ricocheted around the tight space and further jarred the nerves of everyone present. The relatives and friends kept turning up, so the nurse had to fight through the red-eyed crowd propping up the walls in the hall to summon us for our visit. No-one made eye contact and there was not enough room to collapse and grieve properly.

The doctors had told me earlier that the second series of tests had been performed, yielding the same results as the first. Now the machines would be switched off, the procedure would begin for an examination by the coroner, which would be followed by an operation to remove whatever organs she would donate. Since I'd been told that there was virtually no hope from the start, even though this news rang out the literal death knell for Mum—she was now legally dead and at the mercy of medical protocol—the news brought as much relief as grief. Tucked up the previous night searching for sleep in Bart's spare bedroom, I came to the conclusion that, if you scraped away the layers of grief and the lifetime of memories associated with the very sight of her, if it was possible to look at her objectively, lying there buried in her hospital bed, it didn't really feel like she had been 'there' at any point since I arrived. I'd wanted her to be, but she wasn't. I began to realise that, rather than being about to embark on a journey, she had probably already left. A body kept warm and inflated by machines is just that—a body. If that was the case, then it was easier to believe that she was in a better place, feeling no pain. Maybe she was gearing up to step back into the revolving door for another turn.

The four of us made our way through the crowd, washed our hands and visited Mum again. Was she looking more pallid as the days passed or was it just the fluorescent lighting, or my fragile state of mind? All the grief outside, and the realisation that this might be my final farewell suddenly hit me. The walls were closing in; I couldn't avoid thinking about what was next for her and how I was supposed to be the one to support this 50-year-old virtual stranger who was all but laying claim over the latter part of her life. I barely held on while Dave and Helen stepped forward to pay their pre-emptive respects. When it was my turn, all I could do was rub her hand, let the tears flow and whisper, 'It's not fair' until I ran out of air.

An indeterminate period later I came to and Dave, Helen and I shuffled back out to the waiting area while Kevin stayed to say his final farewells. I was given a choice for one more visit but I had said everything I wanted to say and thought everything I could think.

It was the thought that she was already gone—possibly the truth, possibly created to help me cope—that leant against the feeling of loss and helped keep me upright.

On the other side of the seesaw, sat Kevin.

That morning, he had mentioned that he had a confession to make. He told me that he and my mum had been fighting at the time of her accident.

A small detail? Yes and no.

He said that the red wine had been flowing, voices had been raised, things had become heated and the argument had concluded with him shutting himself in his bedroom, leaving Mum out in the hall. A shouting match through the door ensued and the end result was Kevin punching a hole in the door. The way Kevin told it, midway through the fracas, Mum had stopped shouting and he, still in the bedroom had waited a while, calming down. He'd heard a strange noise during that time, which he later realised was her hitting the carpeted floor, but with all the crashing and bashing that had been going on, he didn't think anything of it.

When he opened the door, she was lying on the floor, tongue lolling, making 'a weird gagging sound'. He then dragged her into his bedroom and started CPR.

Oh, righto then. Fine. No problem.

It was a plausible story, but even though he clearly felt terrible about it and honked into his hanky several more times during its telling, the journalist in me immediately wanted more information. In Kevin's version of events, there was no blame to be attributed, and he was to be thanked for his valiant efforts at CPR, but since this was the only version of events that would ever be available where did this leave me, and where did this put him?

And I thought my day couldn't get any more upsetting. Silly me.

Kevin went on to mention that the Victor Harbor police had told him not to go on any long trips in the near future and had said something about not going into Mum's bedroom until they said it was okay.

'What, like it's a crime scene?'

This put a different spin on mentions of the coroner over the last two days. The medicos had said that even though the TV news made it easy to associate the coroner with suspicious deaths, this wasn't necessarily the case. Part of his job was simply to determine the cause of a death when it isn't obvious, and ascertain if there was anything government could do to prevent this kind of death occurring again. My alarm bells had stopped ringing at that explanation, but what if there was a more sinister reason the coroner's office was sniffing around? I didn't fully believe this, but the revelation was more than enough to once again throw me out of kilter.

My kilter was even more askew when the friendly coroner folk told me I had one more grisly job to perform. I had to identify 'the body'. Just procedure, they said, maybe a couple of questions.

The CCU was quieter this time, and inside there were two uniformed police waiting at the nurses' station opposite my mum's bed. They were from the coroner's office and were obviously schooled in the art of sensitivity. I was hoping for a short, sharp, look-confirm-leave scenario, but it was not to be. The officers were sorry for my loss and sorry they had to ask all these questions. But ask them they did. Lots of them, some involving Kevin. Then, also with great sensitivity, they asked me to turn and look into her bay. Sure enough, there my mum lay, this time without the benefit of breathing tubes, drip lines and monitors.

So that was it then. It was all over.

That night at Bart's, Liz rang to tell me that she had booked a flight for the next day, and I have rarely been more relieved. Although the baby was our number one priority, she was halfway through her second trimester, so flying posed no real risk, and the gravity of the situation was threatening to crush me. I was shuffling around like a human husk and I needed her support more than ever.

I met Liz at the airport the next morning and I nearly cried with relief. I had tried to maintain that everything was under control and I didn't need her help, but I think the desperate edge on my voice carried over the phone line well enough.

She turned a page in the saga. Now I had someone in my corner, someone to check with to make sure what I was feeling and doing was reasonable, and someone there to catch me if I went into freefall, although she wasn't allowed to do any other heavy lifting.

I hadn't known if I could face walking into Mum's house without Liz, but with her there I was looking forward to the change of scenery the bus trip south would bring. I had to get away from the grief-soaked walls of that hospital.

The hospital had other ideas.

Could we come in again and collect Mum's jewellery?

So, the refreshing bus ride away from the grief had to wait as Liz and I, inveterate doers of the right thing, trooped back to the hospital.

An hour later we were on our way to Victor Harbor.

Kevin was there in Red Fred to pick us up at the bus stop and soon we were back in the house I had spent the previous sixteen years of holidays in, the person who made it my home away from home replaced by a caretaker interloper.

Liz and I wandered around, still not quite believing what had happened, and the enormity of the task that lay ahead of us. Just to think about cleaning and clearing the house seemed like a disloyal act, as if we had given up on her too soon and already moved on. We were barely game enough to look in drawers and open cupboards but the scale of the job was enormous and we only had about two weeks in which to do it. Liz had booked Bob and Matilda into kennels for a fortnight and she wasn't working, so I couldn't afford to have much longer off.

On our first night in what was still Mum's house, it all weighed heavily on us. Kevin was still ensconced in the end bedroom and the master bedroom was a crime scene, or the next best thing, so we threw a mattress down on the floor in the computer room and collapsed with exhaustion, as much escaping Kevin as trying to sleep.

We left the light on as we chatted wearily to make sense of the last few days. In low bedtime tones Liz mentioned the baby, how much my mum was looking forward to its arrival and how proud she would have been. Then something odd happened. The light in the room flickered on and off, more quickly than would be possible with a light switch, for perhaps five seconds. In sixteen years I had never seen any light flicker that way in the house, and it didn't happen again for the rest of our stay. Maybe that was the supernatural thumbs-up.

For the next two days we tried to focus and make a start on sorting out the house. We found homes for much of

Mum's menagerie and made a reluctant start on a systematic clearing of the drawers and cupboards. Kevin was in and out of the house all the while, sobbing constantly and relating stories about Mum as if Liz and I had only just met her. Even though he would wisely make himself scarce much of the time, Liz and I needed some privacy to decompress from the events of the last few days.

After a series of increasingly blunt hints, eventually he got the message and disappeared to stay with a friend. We bid him a heartfelt goodbye—I was truly grateful for what he had done for my mum—but his role raised too many questions and Liz and I were too emotionally spent to bear the weight of his pain as well. Finally we could breathe.

We had to start thinking about a funeral. We decided to hold it at a tiny local Uniting Church that Mum had rediscovered a few years before. It was in an area of town known as Yilki and the female minister and small congregation there had provided lots of support to Mum during that time and she had made plenty of friends. She had even enlisted much of the congregation's support in helping her pray for the safe arrival of her grandchild. Hopefully those prayers would be enough.

On 6 January a crowd gathered at the tiny stone Yilki church for the funeral of Jennifer Lamb. Initially, the funeral was to be a day later, but since that was my birthday I had it changed. It would be no kind of birthday anyway, but I wanted to separate the two events, if only for my own future mental health.

The building was barely big enough for 100 mourners, but there was a friendly edge to the sombre mood, as most of those attending were locals who stood about chatting respectfully before being herded inside. Liz and I sat in the front row, almost within touching distance of the small table that held a photo of Mum, some candles and rose petals. At the door the guests were offered packets of memorial seeds, something to plant in their gardens to remember my mother by.

The ceremony went as well as it could. I had found the time to write a eulogy that expressed some insight into Mum's life and it seemed to be well received, as were the hymns and a song about a dove sung by a local guitarist, who valiantly tried to get through to the end before breaking down.

Afterwards we all trooped back to a local pub for the wake—certainly something that she would have insisted on—and whiled away several hours reminiscing, philosophising and even sharing a laugh. I was so pleased that there was an upbeat mood in the gathering, and I had such a good time chatting with her friends about her life and my genesis that I felt almost guilty. But the last thing Mum would have wanted for her last knees-up was a sober affair where a sense of reverence was observed out of obligation. She was not one to stand on ceremony so we stood by the bar, let the drinks flow and celebrated her life.

Four days later, with the house that much tidier and Liz and I that much wearier, we drove into the city for her cremation. The first stop was the funeral home, where I was again asked to view her body, laid out in an open coffin in the building's chapel.

In a trip filled with low points, this was the nadir. The sight of her was so distressing that I immediately knew I had to start actively forgetting it. She was laid out in the silvery lace dress we had provided, so tiny in the giant padded coffin with the top half open. This was all as expected, but there was something wrong with her face...

This destroyed me. Whatever 'work' had been done to her, whatever removing and packing and preserving and rearranging had taken place, had distorted the skin of her face, especially near her mouth, to give her the look of something masquerading as human but not quite getting there. She had the stretched, manic mouth of Jack Nicholson's Joker after the nerve gas took effect. The make-up couldn't hide it and I couldn't take it. I quickly moved away and sat towards the back of the room to pay my respects.

Afterward, while talking with the funeral director, just before heading to the cremation, we finally scored a lighter moment. The woman, in the gentle manner required by her job, approached us and produced a small plastic vial.

She didn't quite know how to put it. 'We...found this piece of jewellery, of your mother's and, well, we thought you may have wanted it.' It took a moment to realise what that tiny thing rattling around in the bottom of the plastic vial was: a barbell for a nipple piercing.

Initially I was slightly disturbed, but when the funeral director retreated Liz and I had a good snigger.

'Kids, you see this barbell through my nipple right here? Jason Jnr, get your finger out of your nose when I'm talking to you—this barbell had been in the family for six generations before we nearly lost it when your Grandma died. Good thing that funeral director was on the ball...'

Even in death Mum had the ability to shock us and lighten the moment.

That afternoon we followed the funeral car to the crematorium in the centre of Adelaide's Centennial Park cemetery, and were ushered into a squat brick building in the middle of the cemetery's spectacular gardens. We took a seat in the small room inside, which was divided from the rest of the building by a small door and floor-to-ceiling glass wall. Our crematory host stayed with us and breezily discussed what was about to happen, along with the weather, the fact that he had just shaved his beard off after many years—and he may have even covered international affairs. Clearly he did this almost every day, but we were more confronted by the procedure. And even more confronted when the coffin I had visited an hour earlier was wheeled in on a metal trolley by an attendant and lined up with one of the shining steel ovens. Our MC apologised that we wouldn't be able to view the process in extreme close-up, but the closest oven was on the blink. But we were more than welcome to push the 'go' button that would activate the conveyer belt.

I said no, that was okay, so he finally left us to our privacy and behind the glass the conveyer belt soon whirred smoothly into life. My mother's coffin made its way toward the oven, and we said our tearful goodbyes. As it approached the furnace, the rollerdoor rose and then closed and the coffin disappeared forever.

Liz and I looked at each other. It was a feeling of release, but a strangely anticlimactic end to her physical presence. In the centre of a huge expanse of rolling rose gardens, she had disappeared like a magician's box-in-a-box illusion, gone in one slow, short journey.

Still, even before the incinerator fired up, we were pretty sure she was already in the air above us looking down.

Rest in peace, Jennifer Lamb. We will never forget you.

TRIMESTER III: REVENGE OF THE BUMP

Four months before Liz's due date, our clan was already expanding faster than her burgeoning bump. In mid-January 2005 Liz and I and our dogs Bob and Matilda welcomed two interlopers into the family fold: my mum's dog Ollie and cat Smudge. On our return from South Australia we met them at a freight door in Brisbane Airport and our first parental duty was to load the two cages—one containing an apoplectic barking dog—onto a trolley and concentrate on turning invisible as we trundled them through the terminal to the carpark.

We had devoted some thought to how we'd introduce a newborn into a two-hound house, but another dog and cat hadn't been on the blueprint. We'd already exposed

Boober and Tilster to plenty of babies and they had done very well, aside from Bob's slightly unsavoury fondness for the smell of breast milk. In the following two months, however, we would find ourselves at the centre of an unexpected and fascinating behavioural experiment in which two calm dogs are joined by a third excitable dog to see how many laps around the lounge room it takes before their owners list them all on eBay.

For a few weeks after we'd expanded to a family of six I wandered around the house and went to work not quite knowing where I fitted into the world anymore. I waded in to my work and chores mainly as a way to fill in the day, rather than as a means of actually being useful. The emptiness left in the wake of Mum's death was starting to hit home in earnest and when the furniture and personal effects we'd sent up from her place arrived, all I could manage to do was stash them under the house to deal with later. I was still incredibly excited in the lead-up to the final stages of Liz's pregnancy, but any good cheer or optimism seemed like a betrayal to my mother. As the months passed, though, gradually I began to see that to not make the most of the pregnancy that Mum had been so focused on would be infinitely more disloyal. By all accounts one minute your baby is just a twinkle in your IVF scientist's eye, the next they're thinking about sharing their own DNA with drunken friends at parties. I vowed to enjoy his/her early days before they flew by.

At that point, our bump's very early days consisted mainly of visits to Dr Bob the obstetrician, and hanging there in limbo while Liz and I crossed our digits and stared at May 10 on the calendar. As each weekly visit to George Jetson MD passed he would shake my hand warmly and I'd settle in next to his desk as he took Liz across to his exam bench, squeezed goo onto her belly and ran an audio probe over it. After a short burst of static (was that a snippet of easy listening hits?), a strong, fast heartbeat would squawk out of the audio device. Occasionally he'd take a while to zero in on the foetal heartbeat and our pulses would outrun our baby's until that rhythmic *whish-whoosh-whish-whoosh* filled the room.

During one visit Dr Bob felt Liz's belly and mentioned that our baby was sitting right-side up with its head under Liz's ribs and possibly folded up with its feet near its face. This was a bit awkward but the doc said that over the next couple of months our little one should spin around and engage its head in Liz's pelvis. We went through to his ultrasound room for a good look and, sure enough, the baby was doubled up, practically sucking on its toes. I suggested that maybe we'd better confirm the baby's sex, just, you know, so that we knew where we were but there was nothing doing. Ever since our twenty-week scan, I'd wanted confirmation of the medical opinion that we were to have a daughter, but we could never quite get a decent look. After all we'd come through, I suppose I was after some kind of certainty in the outcome of this process, but it seemed we were more likely to score a signed 8x10 glossy of Bigfoot than a decent gawk at our baby's genitalia.

•

Late January was the start of an intense period of visitor action at our place. Our friends and family were keen to get in quick or be caught in the whirlwind of nappies, formula and upchuck that early May would bring, and they came in droves.

Liz's brother and sister-in-law flew in for a quick visit and, like many of our southern visitors, were happy to park their carcasses in the hammock and doze on the deck. They were soon followed by friends from Newcastle and then the momentous visit of Derek and May, all the way from the UK. Our wives couldn't agree on which one of us boys was the more idiotically excited at the prospect of the visit but I had been planning activities for months, even sitting for my boat licence so I could slip on a skipper's hat and take us out for a day of fishing and aquatic urination on Moreton Bay. Just to sweeten the deal, our mate Handy Andy flew up from Sydney to rendezvous for a good old-fashioned boys' weekend, er, with girls.

We blokes knew it would be our last semi-debauched get-together before the long hook of parenthood came out of the wings and dragged me off the late-night stage once and for all, so we were keen to fit in as much as possible and we only had a few days to do it in.

To kick off proceedings, we decided to devote a Friday night and a few trillion brain cells to closely studying a vast array of monk-based tipples at a Belgian beer café in the city. Things started sedately enough, but before we could say 'I can't feel my head' it was 3am and we had been sucked into the tractor beam of the city's casino.

Those who live in capital cities will know what I mean. Why is it that one minute you are heading out for the mythical 'few quiet ones' and the next you find yourself under a blackjack table with your shirt on backwards singing 'Bust A Move' while tying patrons' shoelaces together? Forget a cure for cancer, our research dollars need to be devoted to *this* riddle of the ages.

Unfortunately I had done my civic duty and given blood earlier in the day, so there was far less blood in my alcohol system than was healthy. Yep, it was the blood donation. Or perhaps 'food poisoning'. In any event, my turn as wise old salty Captain Sealegs the next day was not as successful as it could have been. It was successful in that I managed to pilot our boat out of a protected harbour and into a protected non-harbour area, but unsuccessful with respect to the captain remaining upright and doing anything bar clinging to the deck and focusing on the swaying horizon. I'm pleased to say that, in my absence, there were many capable crewmates ready to step in and run the boat aground, fail to light the barbecue and remark that 'there's something wrong with the anchor thing', so things still went to plan.

Looking back, this final mini-rebellion before I was anointed a dad was more successful than even I could have hoped.

During my self-pickling quest, Liz and I had noticed that, while Derek was at his guzzling best during our friends' stay, May was seemingly uninterested in alcohol, and were we imagining things or was she also avoiding shellfish? We questioned the two of them and they

explained it away, but I was still suspicious. The only
way to really tell would be to hold her down and upend
a cheeky bottle of semillon over her mouth. It was a
good plan, but I was pretty sure Derek would shove his
wife aside and get his mouth under it before a drop hit
the floor. He hates waste, that one.

We would later learn that May was indeed pregnant,
along with two other couples we knew. The baby onslaught
of our pre-pregnancy days continued, but this time (touch
wood) we were heading the charge.

Over the next few months the visitors kept coming,
and there was still no indication that they had come to
see me. Most had been drawn by one of the seven natural
wonders of the reproductive world, Liz's bump, and so
many made the pilgrimage that I was on the verge of
asking for some kind of tourism grant to turn our backyard
into coach parking. *Central Australia has Uluru, southeast
Queensland has Liz's bump. Sort of the same shape but
on the side. Climbing now forbidden due to objections
from traditional owners.* The exception to the pilgrimage
was Bart, who I was glad to see under happier circumstances than last time. True to form, he took some interest
in Liz's bloom of pregnancy but a far greater interest in
cultivating his own beer baby, with plenty of help from
those ever-reliable drunk Belgian monks.

It was about this time that I felt my first baby-kick.
I had been aiming all manner of goofy voices at Liz's
belly since she'd started to report movement down there,
and after a mere two months of CB radio-speak (*Daddy*

to baby, come in baby) and scratching Liz's tummy with my chin I was rewarded with a crabby kick in reply.

A kick in the eye. Is there anything more beautiful? It was a powerfully tangible and physical sign of life, and surely one of the warmest bonding experiences between a dad and his daughter.

It has often been said that you need a licence to drive a car or catch a fish, but any idiot can be a parent. Even though the laws differ in many states, after some investigation I can confirm that this cliché is true—our fair nation is littered with idiot parents. To escape this cycle of stupidity, Liz enrolled us in a four-week Preparation For Parenting class run by our maternity hospital. Given that the sum total of our baby knowledge could easily be scrawled on the back of one of those bits of paper you get in a fortune cookie, in crayon, these parenting titbits would form our major grounding in the whole baby-popping process. As long as they taught us how to hold a baby and change a nappy and the etiquette involved in handing cigars around the birth ward, I figured I would be happy.

We arrived on our first night to find a friendly midwife in front of twenty-five 30-somethings arranged in a semi-circle of chairs.

'Those of you with pillows, if you're after Lamaze, you're in the wrong place. We don't teach that in Australia,' she said, by way of getting-to-know-you chitchat. 'We figure if you got this far you already know how to breathe.' Pause for gales of laughter. We didn't know what Lamaze was, only that the pamphlet had said to bring a pillow. 'What these classes are about is what to expect on your delivery day, coping mechanisms for mums and partners to get you through the birth, and a little bit about how to deal with your new baby.'

And that's what they taught us, more or less. Over four Monday nights we played awkward getting-to-know-you games, learned about the different stages of labour (as far as I could tell: intermittent excruciating pain, constant excruciating pain, pain beyond anything you can currently imagine, and Incredible Hulk mode), reviewed the physiology of the birth process and we blokes learned what we could do to make the process more bearable for our partners (answer: anything she bloody wants). We learned massage techniques, how to gently suggest different birthing positions, shower therapy (yes, bring your boardies, boys), the power of calming or motivating music, and the all-encompassing A–Z method. This was a powerful technique we blokes could use to remember 26 separate ways to ease the pain of our ponderous partners. 'E' is for eye contact, 'B' is for back rub and 'R' is for rocking from foot to foot and humming nervously.

The A–Z technique was all very well but, like the nurse discovered when we put her on the spot, I was sure I'd struggle to come up with more than a fistful. X is for...xylophone accompaniment?

Still, Liz and I were keen. We knuckled down and paid attention and made notes, worried that every other pregnant couple had supped freely from the fountain of baby knowledge while we were still shaking the Coke machine, but we quickly discovered that all the other apprehensive men and rotund women were just as clueless as we were about what came next, which seemed to make Liz happy. Balancing this was the nurse edifying us with a constant stream of horrifying risk factors, as the hospital was legally obliged to do.

In the twenty-first century, caesarean sections are as common as navel rings, people, but it is invasive surgery and one in 1.5 zillion will suffer major complications...

Breech births? Usually hunky-dory, unless your baby's head is too big for your pelvis, which you won't know until it's too late...

But we could help by being supportive. Gone are the days of wives calling the front bar of the Duck and Bucket to inform a new dad of an addition to the family. Now dads are an important member of the birthing 'team', just behind the massage therapist and boundary umpire in order of importance. We had already covered the countless things dads could do to help—therapeutic music, back rubs, supporting the mother-to-be in a hot shower, supplying everything from ice chips to cold flannels to warm flannels to dodging flannels and being screamed at in tongues.

The midwife emphasised this last point, saying that partners should not expect any niceties from their wives while in the throes of birth.

Then she went on to say that mothers-to-be will often desperately need help but be unable to ask for it, or sometimes mean the exact opposite of what they are saying.

'You will have to read her signals and anticipate her needs. Let's say you suggest a different birthing position and she screams "No!" at you. Sometimes "no" means "yes" and you need to persevere.'

Now I was really confused. For fellas, hadn't the 'no means yes' theory been given the thumbs down since those very thumbs became opposable? Until this point I'd been looking forward to the whole birth suite experience. I figured I'd do my best to help out, maintain eye contact and chuck in a smidgin of relaxation breathing for effect, but let's face it, I wasn't the one under pressure. Until now. Now, according to this midwife, at any particular juncture I was expected to have a Rolodex of therapeutic solutions I could draw from to ease the pain of the very person who may be threatening to castrate me if I touched her. Or she may just be kidding, okay?

I began to chew the end of my complimentary pencil.

It was hard to tell whether the classes had made Liz more or less relaxed about the birthing process. Her jaw-clenched smile made many appearances during that period, but it had been pretty much a fixture for the previous twelve months, so the jury was out on that one.

Me, I was a changed man. Before baby school I had been relaxed about the whole affair. One of the benefits of maledom—and I was being reminded of this ad nauseam—was that I was a passenger in the process. I figured I'd hold Liz's hand, rub her back, make sure she was comfortable and dish out ice chips until baby made three. How naïve can a father-to-be be? Now I'd been informed that the whole process hinged on me. I had to read the signs. I had to know what that particular grunt meant. I had to know when to ignore the abuse flying at me and when to act on it. Oh, God! What if I couldn't remember what 'K' was for?

I liked being clueless better.

Meanwhile, our unborn child was proving to be a stubborn little individual. The baby had left it so long to turn and had grown so much that there was very little room left for it to manoeuvre. After being cooked up in a lab, cultivated with drugs, probed, scanned, jabbed and scrutinised throughout every moment of its gestation, it seemed the child was now exerting its authority and maybe exacting a little payback on its pushy parents.

The week before, at about 31 weeks, the doc had examined Liz's belly to gauge the chances of him turning the baby from the outside, but Liz's tum was more like a tom-tom, easily taut enough to drum out a nice reggae rhythm on. Perhaps something by Bunny Wailer. I don't know. It was a testament to Liz's tight tummy muscles, but it meant that there was no turning the baby manually. To add to the little tyke's problems, it was still bent up in half practically munching on its toes, which increased the likelihood of hip problems in its early development. It also robbed the baby of the purchase to spin around.

Doctor Bob told us that a natural breech birth was possible, but the risks of complications were greatly increased, especially for a first-time mother. Firstly, when the baby was doubled over and bum-first, since the bum was smaller than the head, if the baby got halfway out and the doc found the cervix hadn't dilated enough, the baby's head could get stuck inside. This could prove disastrous, oxygen-flow-wise. The doc strongly suggested that if our little cherub didn't turn, Liz should have a c-section (caesarean). She was initially disappointed to miss her chance at having a go at a natural birth, but in the face of very significant risks, there was no way we'd deviate from our medical advice. Besides, you just can't argue with someone called Bob.

Once Liz got used to the idea, she figured that no part of the baby's life had been completely natural so far, so why should the birth be any different? And there were plenty of advantages to a cut-and-run birth. With an appointment about two weeks prior to the full-term date, things are much easier to plan for and there is little chance of a midnight dash to the hospital. The birth itself would also be reduced from indeterminate hours of pain and grief to about fifteen minutes of discomfort, and Liz would have no choice to make about a drug-free delivery. When five layers of tissue are being sliced open with large, gleaming scalpels, drugs are pretty much par for the course. A friend from work had raved about c-sections, keen on the fact he found himself holding his baby soon after the start of the procedure. This sounded good to me, as did skipping the umpteen hours of sweating and cursing and I began to get very comfortable with this quick unzip technique. Of course, it would be a lot more complex than that, but we had virtually no choice, and I'd be up the other end, right?

However, the prospect of a c-section raised the spectre of an old supervillain—the evil Count Anaesthesia. Our doctor recommended a spinal block, which is slightly different to an epidural but would have the same effect, numbing her entire body from roughly the neck down. While it wasn't quite general anaesthesia, it was perhaps cold comfort to her to be only losing control of 80 per cent of her body, rather than the lot. But we both knew she had no choice, and she dealt with her anxiety like a trouper.

Dr Bob pencilled us in for a caesarean section on 29 April. April! As in *next month*!

The days had been ticking down quickly toward 10 May and the ticking was even louder for 29 April.

During a tea break in our next parenting class Liz asked the midwife if there was anything she could do to get our headstrong baby to turn and ready itself to slide down the fleshy escape chute (a technical term). She was still keen to have a crack at a natural birth, and who could blame her? I mean, such an appealing case for it had already been made by the graphic birth video we'd watched in week one of class. I have no problem, in theory, with footage of mothers sweating, heads emerging, fluids flowing and all the other visceral elements of the wondrous miracle of birth. After all, there was a chance my good wife was about to experience just that. However, watching such footage tends to make me look like I've just eaten a lemon.

But I felt it was important to face up to the reality, so, I am proud to say, I winced and barely flinched my way through the video, although I thought the guy next to me was going to launch his dinner into the circle for group discussion. I was glad I stuck with it, in the end. With any luck, this was as up close and personal as I would get to the miracle of birth, so watching the video right through felt like a rite of passage. I was so impressed with the mother-meets-baby dénouement that I was thinking about scarfing down a few cricket balls, just to get a taste of such an uplifting experience.

For turning breech babies the midwife suggested a couple of yoga moves involving Liz sticking her bum in the air, the theory being that the baby's own weight was helping it 'sit' down in the pelvis in the breech position. If Liz simulated a little zero-gravity in the womb it might free up the little mite to do a spin. This was all very well, but Liz found later that she could hold these positions only as long as she could stand every millilitre of blood in her body taking up residence in her facial tissue.

By mid-March, a chest of drawers we had sent up from Mum's place was close to half-full of baby clothes. We were yet to invest in a single jumpsuit ourselves, but every day the postman would deliver another delicately knitted jacket from Aunty Bev or consignment of never-worn hand-me-downs from one of Liz's fertile friends. The fashion colour schemes were mostly unisex lemon, white and green, but I could tell it was all Liz could do not to race down to the nearest Newborns 'R' Us and swipe the credit card red-raw stocking up on hot pink micro-fashions. If she bought enough pink it would have to be a girl, right?

The weeks were flying past and it seemed as if we were seeing Dr Bob so much that we should start calling him uncle. During weekly checkups, Liz would submit to the audio probe routine and we would both smile at the insistent heartbeat hammering away inside her. In contrast to every other period in our child's creation, Liz's last trimester seemed to be slipping past in a refreshingly routine manner. Routine, that is, aside from the fact that the baby was still right-side up and folded up like an ironing board, steadfastly refusing to budge.

Smudge the daredevil feline was missing. We'd arrived home from a parenting class one night to find three dogs mindless with glee but no sleek grey cat sliding between our legs. Even though she was not one to hang around the back door pawing her dinner bowl, at the end of the day she would always leap down out of the pergola, or appear from under someone's house to demand dinner. But this time we called and tapped a can in the Smudge-approved manner to no avail. No tinkling bells or suspicious rustling sounds—nothing.

The next morning, still no Smudge, so we widened the search and made a sickening discovery. Our beautiful feline friend was lying bloated in a gutter outside the house, obviously knocked down by a car that had not even bothered to stop. We were more crushed than she was.

As I dug a hole in the front garden and wrapped her stiff body in a towel, it felt like we, the custodians of

Mum's beloved pets, had failed her. Deep down we knew it wasn't really our fault—the bells we added to her collar had stopped her catching wildlife but there was nothing we could do about her love of roaming the neighbourhood—but it was difficult to apply this logic through the tears.

Mum and now her cat. Enough already!

April 2005 was the month that everything would come to a head.

Somewhere along the way the year had ceased to be 2005 AD and become 2005 BB (Before Baby). Our whole existence was now focused not on enjoying our final weeks of freedom, but madly sprinting around to get things done BB.

Since Liz and I got back from South Australia last time, there had been another distasteful chore hanging over my head, and time was running out to get it finished BB. There was still a world of work to be done at Mum's house. Whether we wanted to rent it or sell it, it needed cleaning out and we'd only just scratched the surface of the world's largest mountain of knick-knacks.

In other news, Liz's parents had decided to move up to Brisbane to be closer to their first grandchild. Since the slavering pack of canine chaos cutting a swathe of destruction through our living room was just as fierce as ever, it was decided that Ollie needed to move in with the in-laws in Sydney, which didn't seem like a betrayal because they'd soon be living within walking distance and we'd see plenty of them and plenty of my old furry mate.

Oh, and there was the small matter of a person to create at the end of the month. Well, sort of like a person, but smaller.

In the first week of April I jetted down to South Australia to relive all the joyous memories from last time. I hired a ute in Adelaide and took the south road down to Victor Harbor in glorious autumn weather. With the window open, the wind in my nostril hairs and the McLaren Vale wine region flashing past it was almost like I was off on a weekend fishing jaunt or a spot of carefree outdoor self-flagellation, rather than a miserable mission to dispose of the majority of my dead mother's possessions. When Barry Servo Attendant struck up a conversation to ask what I was up to in my hire ute, what was I supposed to say? It was just easier to mumble something about a holiday and leave it at that.

Standing at Mum's front door with the key in my hand, it was anything but easy. I entered, and the atmosphere struck me like a frying pan in the face. There were too many memories, too many knick-knacks—the tiny stuffed lambs on the kitchen windowsill, the bathroom basin stacked with fragrant individual soaps 'borrowed' from hotels, the little container of marbles on hand for visiting kids. It all added up to a seemingly insurmountable mountain of sadness.

After much soul-searching and encouragement from Liz (who was on the verge of defying doctor's orders and jumping on a plane to help) I forced myself to knuckle down and make a start, and things got a lot easier. I worked my guts out for a week preparing for the world's biggest garage sale, packing trinkets in boxes, working from room to room and pining for Liz, our unborn baby and unruly dogs.

Question to self: Can I really sell a lifetime's worth of her accumulated possessions to strangers for next to nothing?

Answer: I have no fucking choice, do I?

What with the funeral, legal bills, airfares and the cost of sending up to Queensland all the items we wanted to keep, the bills were mounting as fast as the bric-a-brac in her backyard. It seemed like yet another betrayal, but I was sure Mum would have seen the financial necessity behind my actions, so I pressed on with my sorting and stacking. Five boxes of glassware, ten boxes of books. How much on the dining suite? Are these plates in a set? Small plants $5, large plants $10—everything negotiable.

After five days of back-melting toil, I was beating off the second-hand dealers with a stick and watching them wade through the giant skip bin outside. Mum would have been proud at such committed scrounging.

In Saturday's first light the bargain-hunters were virtually kicking the door in to get at the goodies and, with the help of various friends and neighbours, by midday the bones had been picked out of the sale. Three-quarters of Mum's possessions were gone. All day I'd pictured her standing over the scene, tearing her hair out as her favourite yoga book/birdbath/garden hose/ sandwich maker was virtually given away, but I gritted my teeth and haggled on. All I could do was push on and try not to think about it. I'd been doing that a lot lately.

With the sale done, that night I blew off some steam at one of the local pubs with Bart and Glen who'd come down from Adelaide. At three in the morning, frightening the local teens with our liturgical dance moves at the local nightclub, I stopped on the sticky dance floor and thought of Mum. We had spent many a torturous evening together in the place, me in my late teens trying to pretend I wasn't with her while she whooped it up and clawed me back onto the dance floor. I swear I spun through my next revolution of the 'sprinkler' dance with a tear in my eye. Suddenly I realised that I had been handed the torch of public mortification and charged with the grave responsibility of embarrassing a whole new generation of unsuspecting youth. Moonwalking to the bar to seal my resolution with a toast, I vowed not to let Mum down.

Back at home base, despite my threat to hold my breath until I turned blue, the clock continued to tick and the pressure continued to mount. Assuming our stubborn little offspring didn't turn—and it'd need a tiny ice-axe and a kilo of pig fat to pull it off now—we had two weeks to go before B day, an empty 'nursery', no pram, no car seat and (gasp) no poignant 'Baby On Board' sign for the car. Like her expectations of married life, I could tell Liz's soft-focus images of us transferring our cherub from the hospital into a delicately frilled bassinet in a tastefully decorated nursery were fading rapidly. In their place: the stark reality of a bare nursery, bare fridge and barely any time to get everything done.

So we did what we always do. We made to-do lists and worked ourselves into a frenzy to get to the end of them, starving ourselves of the chance to relax, breathe and enjoy the moment. Because that's just the kind of zany folk we are.

The major project—the downstairs study—hadn't been touched and we had to prioritise what we could hope to get done in time. The first item on the list was baby furniture, so we trooped off to our local Snookums's World O' Baby Stuff and prudently purchased only enough gear to cover us in the event that our baby unexpectedly split into quads on delivery. As we walked in swiping our credit card across all point-of-sale devices within reach and making canny shopping comments such as 'I don't know what it is, but we'll have seven' and 'I forgot to look at the price tag', the staff welcomed us with open arms. They didn't even object when I embarked on a series of impromptu stroller side-impact tests, although I thought I saw one shop assistant sneak around behind me brandishing a particularly hefty rattle.

Pretty soon the helpful staff had serviced all our superfluous baby merchandise needs and they even helped us stack boxes onto our car until it resembled a giant game of Jenga.

Then, armed with just a Phillips-head screwdriver, half a roll of sticky tape and a liberal dose of rat cunning, I set about assembling it all.

•

After three years of waiting, our precious baby was almost within our grasp. He or she was right here ... right *there*. I could feel it, I'd seen it, heard its heart beat many times and even communicated with it, boxing-style, by poking it in the head through Liz's belly and getting a kick in return, but our baby was still five thin layers of tissue and seventeen light years away from us. There was a mere ten, no, wait, nine ... eight days to go and I found myself in bed at night, staring at the wall wondering if there was anything more I could do to bring it to us safely. Had we covered every contingency? Had we missed anything? Surely we couldn't get this far and fail? (Reach out from under the covers and touch wooden bed frame. Continue staring into darkness.)

In the last days of the pregnancy, the final hurdle was almost dragged a tad closer.

It was our last visit to Doctor Bob, and there seemed no hope for little baby Davis to spin around and come down that fleshy slip'n'slide of its own accord. I was even prepared to dangle sweet treats near the opening, but I didn't mention this to the doctor. All I could do was sit back and listen once more to my child's heartbeat and silently bemoan the fact that I wouldn't confirm its sex before the birth.

On our way out of his office, Doctor Bob mentioned in an alarmingly offhand manner that, because of a long weekend issue he may have to move Liz's c-section forward two days. We were shuffling toward the twenty-ninth so delicately balanced on the knife edge between excitement and fear that even such a small whiff of change threatened to send us into freefall. As the doc diddled with his diary, his secretary wielding pencil and eraser with not a care in the world, Liz and I exchanged silent looks of panic. Six days' time had a nice ring to it. Four, not so peachy. But then he looked again and found he was booked solid on the Wednesday (oh, golly, *damn* the luck) and we were pencilled back in for Friday 29 April.

Like baseballers sliding in to home plate to beat the throw, Liz's parents packed up their car and dogs and moved up from Sydney and into the next suburb mere hours before they were to become grandparents.

All eyes were on us and the saga was building up to a small (but hopefully perfectly formed) finish.

CHICK RAFFLE

For me, 29 April 2005 started like every other day, in the morning. At the insistence of an unrelenting bladder and a couple of even less relenting hounds, I drifted into a semi-conscious state at around 6am, stumbled zombie-like to the bathroom for a groggy can't-miss sit-down wee and then to the back door to let the scratching dogs in. As usual they joyfully flayed the skin from my legs until we all trooped off back to bed.

When I resurfaced, Liz had been up for at least an hour, as per usual. Faced with such a daunting day, I must admit I'd expected to find her feverishly polishing the silver or just huddled in a corner, mumbling to herself and combing her head bald. But no, she was a picture of calm efficiency, collecting clothes for her six days in hospital, organising paperwork and readying the house for a dangerously long stint as Jase's Pad O' Filth. I made cheery small talk while circling warily, looking for cracks in her calm countenance that would reveal the molten magma of terror beneath, but found little. She did have a bit of a weep at a poignant Michael Bublé song (it was about 'a new day, a new life' you see) on breakfast TV but she recovered well. She'd be fine until we got to the hospital, she said. Bravo.

As for me, the more consciousness I gained, the more excited I was becoming. A single cup of caffeine would put me in danger of turning (through a process of spontaneous skivvification) into the fifth Wiggle. Now we were delivering via caesarean there was less pressure on me. To hear the doctors explain it, there would be so many people in the theatre it sounded like I'd be standing in line just to pat Liz's hand.

Like Liz, I thought it would have been incredible to sweat and strain through the whole process—to lose hope and then make progress and triumph after hours of torture, and finally hold our beautiful child in our arms, the three of us utterly spent. But skipping the end part was fine too. In fact, while it would have been an unforgettable memory and something we would cherish for a lifetime, I was more than a little relieved to be waiting in the express checkout. I felt, at this point, the less anguish, the better for both of us.

With everything planned, I spent the morning helping with chores and throwing in copious amounts of soothing smiles and calming back rubs. We'd been told to be at the hospital at about 1.30pm for a consultation with our anaesthetist, so there was even time for a calming dog walk. Strolling along the sands of Moreton Bay on that balmy early-autumn morning—our last morning as a two-human, two-pooch family—I looked over as the sun caught in the hair of my beautiful, distended, contented wife and wildly mad dogs and I had a moment. *Am I worthy of anything more? Some out there have nothing, and I have all of this, all of these people (I must remember to email the dogs to inform them they're not human) who love me. Am I pushing my luck to ask for a healthy baby too?* When Bob dropped his ball at my feet for only the 245th time I mentally pinned this pessimistic Post-it note to it and hurled it as far as I could across the peaceful sand flats of the bay.

To prepare for the operation, Liz's nil-by-mouth regime started at 11am. After the obligatory dog wash, she got a snack in just before deadline then washed herself with a Medi-sponge soaked in yellow antiseptic solution and dressed for a long period of lying about. By the time we'd checked everything, loaded the car and gently explained the situation to the dogs, it was time to head off into the great medical unknown.

Over the years, when I'd imagined the drive to the hospital for the birth of our first child, I'd come up with images far removed from this reality. Firstly, I always imagined it would be three in the morning and Liz would be screeching at me from the passenger seat, unmentionable fluids rushing between her fingers as she tried to hold the baby in while I floored it, occasionally even touching down on all four wheels at once. What I did not envision was this sedate, thoroughly planned daytime trip during which we had time to pause and admire the weather, discuss national affairs and remark several times that, 'This just seems weird, doesn't it?'

Twenty-five carefully planned, speed-limited minutes later and we had pulled into the leafy surrounds of Brisbane's North West Private Hospital. We were bang on time and set about gathering Liz's gear to check in and get settled before the pain-go-away man turned up.

Maybe it was the holiday Monday that week or it could have been the bedroom frisson generated by the Athens Olympics beach volleyball coverage exactly nine months earlier, but at the maternity ward it was spawning room only. There was nary a bed spare in the place. Despite tales of double-bedded rooms and approved sleep-overs for dads, northern Brisbane was in the grip of a baby boom in that last week of April, so we were ushered into a twin room, going halves with whoever was behind blue-green privacy curtain number one.

Actually, the room's other half was living in a decidedly more cramped area than we had, and from the nurses' frequent visits and the dulcet tones of a grizzling newborn, it sounded like our neighbour was struggling through her first or second day as a mum.

We'd scored the half of the room next to the window and had more than enough room to swing a cat. The bed had an electric hand control, which I quickly dis-covered opened up infinite positioning possibilities for viewing the TV mounted on the wall above it. If it weren't for the breastfeeding and nipple care videos on channel 1,

I may have elbowed the patient out of the bed and moved in myself. Still, on second thoughts, you can never be too careful with your nipples. I made a mental note to check mine when there was no threat of a nurse bursting in.

We stowed Liz's stuff and sat around waiting on our anaesthetist. And we waited, and we waited, and I had a cup of tea and twiddled my thumbs and waited. Nurses came fussing in and out to prep Liz and get her changed into a green surgical smock (this one chastely fastened at the side for a reduced crack count), but there was no sign of the doctor.

At three o'clock he was still a no-show. We'd chipped almost two hours off the mountain of waiting time until our 5pm surgery slot, but sitting in a hospital room spinning your surgical wristband has the potential to mess with even the calmest demeanour. Despite the anticipation and crushing silence, Liz was doing an admirable job of keeping her upper lip rigid and her eyes on the prize, and trying not to think of the hole it would be coming through. Aside from explaining what we could expect in the operating theatre not less than half a dozen ways, our frazzled nurses had mentioned that there had been a couple of emergency patients that had pushed us back on the schedule.

When four o'clock was quickly followed by five o'clock, with a special guest appearance by 5.30, we started to wonder if we'd been overlooked. We get that a lot. We're the type of no-fuss people who often get passed over, so much so that in restaurants we're almost at the point where we become spooked by attentive wait staff. In cafés, in queues, in the front bar of any pub we stroll into, we are polite, we don't complain, and therefore quickly cease to exist. I was about to put on my 'excuse me, but we've been here 40 minutes and haven't seen a menu yet' voice—which never fails to strike abject indifference into the hearts of hospitality workers—when a nurse bustled in and announced that we were up.

We said our Hail Marys, sent a mental SMS to Jehovah and swore off pork until further notice. We'd covered all bases and we were ready.

Yet again a nurse arrived to go through a play-by-play for each of us—this time it was a large, walrus-like male version with a rumbling voice and a dry quip for every occasion. After the chat he set about unhooking Liz's bed from its power source and getting her mobile for the trip upstairs.

Whenever anyone is wheeled anywhere on a hospital bed I have a bad habit of daydreaming whimsical *Bedknobs And Broomsticks*-style scenes, which is most unhelpful because the people involved are usually about to have something serious and important cut out, stitched up or replaced at the time and are more in need of quiet reassurance than a few bars from 'Substitutiary Loco-motion'. But I'm proud to say that when my wife was wheeled down the hall on her way to the operating theatre, I managed to focus on the job at hand. When the nurse referred to me as 'Dad' for the first time it snapped me out of my daydream and gave me goose-bumps, once my brain whirred into action and worked out who he was talking to.

Outside the operating suite, Liz's bed and its entourage closed in on the obligatory double doors and I braced for impact. Clearly, standard operating procedure states that you must slam any bed or gurney-like object through such double doors screaming 'Stat!' at anyone you can find, but these nurses weren't playing by the *ER* rulebook. It's far easier and quieter for two nurses to just hold them open, apparently.

Liz was wheeled into a small anteroom outside the operating theatre for yet another briefing while nurse I. M. T. Walrus (koo koo cha-choo) dispatched me to a change room to garb up. The temperature inside the surgery area seemed a couple of degrees cooler than the rest of the hospital, although there may have been other mitigating factors causing my knees to knock as I discarded my regular clothes in favour of blue surgical scrubs. With the operation predicted to take only 10–15 minutes, in less than an hour I would be holding a brand new healthy child (touch wood). It was such a foreign concept that there would have been no chance of my forming the answer 'I'm the father', had I been asked.

But there were a lot of hurdles to leap before we got to the botty-smacking part, if indeed that still happened in this enlightened age. First off, in order to escape from that glorified bathroom, I had to find a pair of pants not formerly used as a scout jamboree mess hall. For some reason all the shirts were of vaguely human proportions but the strides were *huge*. Add to that the paper hat and shoe-covers and I slid out of that change room like a drunken bit player from M. C. Hammer On Ice.

Outside the door to the operating theatre, our swarthy, charming anaesthetist (and part-time photographer) was giving Liz the lowdown on the insertion of her spinal block and the other pharmaceutical assistance he could deliver during the operation. I thought he was going into far too much detail about the risk factors involved. I had brought Liz's portable CD player this far, with a calming disc to distract her from the impending terror (Jack Johnson's *In Between Dreams* was deemed our most chilled chill-out album. One of my old flatmates must have taken my copy of Megadeth's *Killing Is My Business*) but it sat unused on a shelf. The accessory that would find plenty of use, however, was my digital camera, which the anaesthetist triple-checked I had at hand.

Doctor Bob then materialised, much of his George Jetson-ness hidden behind a surgical cap and still more blue scrubs. As usual he left me with a big grin and hearty handshake and disappeared into the theatre. Liz was wheeled in and I was taken around to a rear door to wait until everyone was in place. Through the small window in the door, I could see Liz curled in the foetal position on the operating table, wrapped around nurse Walrus as the anaesthetist bent behind her to insert the needle for the spinal block. By the time I was led into the room by a nurse and put in the low chair next to Liz's head, she was once again divided in two by a green surgical sheet on a frame, she had a drip in her arm, a catheter in her bladder and a needle in her spine. Just the trifecta you need for a really big Friday night.

In the brightly lit room, there was a cast of thousands fussing over various benches, tubes, machines and the patient at the centre of it all. I counted ten people in the room: Doctor Bob, his assistant, our anaesthetist and his assistant, Barry the paediatrician, the paediatric nurse, Nurse Walrus, a surgical nurse, Liz and me. *And baby makes a soccer team.*

The mood in the room was more like Friday night office drinks than Friday night at *All Saints*. Knots of blue-smocked professionals formed and broke apart, chatted, fussed, measured, checked, observed and readied themselves behind scalpels for the next instalment in a long Friday schedule. North of the green sheet, Liz and I made carefully inane chitchat with the anaesthetist and Doctor Bob, discussing important issues such as our eternal search for the right curtains for the baby's room and the rise and rise of digital photography. This passed a few minutes, but Liz was starting to tense up and white-knuckle on the steel edge of panic. I did my best to catch her eye and use the mesmeric breathing technique we'd picked up in our parenting class—you stare deep into each other's eyes and follow your partner's slow, measured breathing (the subliminal birthday gift suggestions are optional)—but she was too far gone. What they don't tell you in birth class is that, with more medical personnel present in the theatre than at even the largest BMW dealership, your good lady wife will also be distracted by said medicos crowding around and asking her if she's okay or messing with her tubes, drips and various medical flim-flam-ery. Happily, just as Liz's eyes really began glazing over with panic, Steve the anaesthetist plugged a syringe into the drip line and announced that the good stuff was on its way.

As well as being a drug kingpin, Steve was North West Hospital's answer to Max Dupain, frequently dragging my camera out of my voluminous pocket for a series of happy snaps in between plugging a cavalcade of pharmaceutical help into my wife's veins. His focus on photography was a little surprising at the time, but I appreciated his efforts later when I downloaded the digital pics to discover beautiful ensemble shots of the docs and me leaning in next to Liz—who was still smiling despite her paralysis—and graphic stills of just what was getting pulled out of where on the other side of the sheet. Those were best saved for after dinner.

When the anaesthetist's assistant verified with an ice cube the point at which Liz was numbed (somewhere just below her chin), the operation could begin. This set me wondering: where did the ice cube come from? Was it a finely calibrated surgical ice cube that came shrink-wrapped in its own plastic case? Maybe Pfizer sold them in three different strengths for all your low-temperature theatre needs. Or maybe it was from someone's Friday night gin and tonic. *That* was the person I needed to find.

While I was in la-la land thinking this through, Doctor Bob announced from the other side of the sheet that he and his team had started the procedure.

Liz told me later that the effect of the anaesthetic on her muscles relaxed her to the point where her fear totally disappeared and she could almost enjoy the experience. At the time, all I remember is looking deep into her eyes, admiring her fortitude and thinking, *It's just as well you're calm, seeing as right now they're carving you up like a Christmas ham.*

We didn't get a lot of commentary from the other side of the sheet, aside from 'the waters are breaking now', but it was soon obvious that there was some serious delving around going on in my wife's insides. I have since researched the anatomical impact of a caesarean section and I can now confidently say that the major organs most affected by the operation are collectively known as 'the gizzards' and they were undergoing plenty of rearrangement. The pulling and pushing from down below was causing Liz to rock around and look less than comfortable, but she handled it with more aplomb than many a temporary quadriplegic.

A bit more pulling and pushing and there was a call of 'I can see the baby'.

Steve the anaesthetist was snapping away over the sheet, so I knew something was up, and then I was asked if I wanted to have a look. It was an odd juxtaposition: the promise of an intimate, gut-churning view of my wife opened up like a zip-lock lunch bag, next to the wondrous sight of our precious new baby. Though I hardly dared, I steadied my shaky knees and poked my head above the sheet.

There were skin colours and blood colours, and a glimpse of a dark, liver-coloured crevasse, but my eyes were transfixed by the pale, waxy little baby being held up in front of me.

Its eyes were mashed shut, its mouth was gaping in shock and its pudgy hands were thrust out in horror. It was a little girl. Messy, indignant, swollen, completely out of her element and trailing an umbilical cord, but definitely a little girl. She was the most beautiful creature I'd ever clapped eyes on.

Welcome to the world, little Rose.

Over the previous few months, when even our all-pervasive superstition couldn't mask the fact that we were a good chance of becoming parents, when we'd checked under every rock, tap-danced on every fertility trapdoor and still remained standing, we'd begun discussing names in earnest. Not for us the fanciful phonetic spellings and kiddies named after fruit; we agreed that we were for good, strong old-fashioned bullet-proof names with maybe a slang or short version for a bit of variety. Several serious suggestions were met with flat rejection—Adolf just doesn't get much of a run these days, does it—and there was plenty of chuckling over the not-so-serious ones. Eventually we decided on Rose for a girl, Rosie around the house, and Benjamin for a boy. We also agreed to each nominate a family name for the middle moniker. When I suggested Jennifer in honour of my mum, Liz applauded the gesture and supplied the male one. As it played out, my name won the chromosomal lottery, and Rose Jennifer Davis was born. My mum, quite appropriately, would have been tickled a rosy shade of pink at the honour.

As I looked at my new daughter being cleaned up for life in the outside world, I could already see a resemblance to Mum. For an electric split-second I caught myself looking forward to rushing into the waiting room downstairs, finding her camped out beside a drift of used Styrofoam teacups and catching her in a teary bear hug. I'd tell her that her granddaughter had the famous Lamb blue eyes, our long fingers and my skinny thumbs. She should ask for more and more details between Kleenexing her eyes raw, and I'd tell her everything I could remember, which wouldn't be enough to sate her.

But, of course, there'd be no hugs. No reunion. Even among the loving fold of Liz's family there would be only a cold seat where, if life was fair, her small frame would have been, already several new friends to the good and organising a pub crawl to celebrate the happy occasion.

I'm not prone to blackouts or bouts of fainting (the missing hours of New Year's Eve 1994 notwithstanding) but I have no idea what transpired during the next 60 seconds in that operating theatre. Did I drop my wife's hand while staring at that yellow, buttery little girl? Possibly. Who even held her up? I have no clue. The emotion of the moment and pounding heartbeat had knocked my eyes offline and only a few deep breaths would reboot them.

The next memory I have is a swimming, clammy one of a red-lipped baby wrapped in a white towel being laid on Liz's chest and then handed to me, although I may have reclaimed these memories from the ready supply of happy snaps I downloaded later that night. In the photos we are all smiles and I look lucid enough, but the endorphins quickly wiped my memory. Hence the importance of snap-happy Steve.

Rose was then handed to the paediatrician and his assistant to be checked over at a warmed, towel-lined little mini-bed. They called me over while they cleaned her up and asked if I'd like to cut the cord. Does the Pope shit in the woods!? Just try to stop me. At this point, unless you have procreated with Elastigirl, the cord has already been cut and you are merely being offered a cord *shortening*, but I wasn't arguing semantics and was handed the little surgical scissors. The baby's umbilical cord was held out and I was told to cut between the two yellow peg clamps. The nurse warned me the sinewy, blue-grey cable was tough, but I sawed my way through it with little trouble and no splashback.

I got in a couple more photos before I took a back seat and was reduced to ducking and weaving behind the staff for a better look. Then I remembered my good lady wife was still paralysed back on the table and went across to sit back down next to her.

Oh.

Jeeeez . . .

Halfway through the second step to the operating table, I felt an emotional dump truck empty its load square on my head. When I looked over at Liz grinning and straining for another glimpse of our child, the words 'she's beautiful' fell from my mouth and the floor tilted. Again, my perverse brain chose that moment to rifle through my mental album of Mum moments; mainly the look on her face and the sound of her voice whenever the subject of this child was raised. In a fraction of a second I could see still frames of our future lined up like dominos waiting to fall, Liz and her mum sharing the baby, the visits, the birthdays, the simple excited chatter they'd share about what Rose had done that day. I would have none of this with my mum. Surrounded by eight bustling professionals, a metre from my wife on one side and my new daughter on the other, for a second I felt my heart shrink with loneliness. I sat down next to Liz and let my tears of loss mix with the tears of elation.

After we shared a moment, it was time for a bit of irony. Liz the Lifesaver was to get a Hole Lot More Out of Life by having her central aperture stitched up.

I was banished to the recovery ward next door to wait, foot tapping, for Rose to arrive. There were a couple of other patients there lying quietly in various states of consciousness, but that was the extent of my cognisance of the outside world. I chatted briefly with a couple of nurses until Dr Barry, our paediatrician, wheeled my daughter in on her small trolley. *My daughter.* She was so new the concept was still very foreign.

As she rolled in, the trumpets sounded, the angels sang and my grin widened. What an entrance.

After some hearty congratulations the man in the smock told me everything was fine, but I begged to differ. She was far from fine. She was perfect and I had to restrain myself from shaking everyone within sight and informing them of the fact, conscious or not. At some point during my afterglow Dr Barry disappeared and I found myself helping his assistant weigh my baby. The digital read-out stopped bang on 3.5kg, which I now know is 7lb 7oz, but in my addled state I converted it to 8lb 8oz in my head. When I later told family and friends the inflated mark, there was much widening of the eyes and many furrowed brows and double takes. But they were too polite to comment and I was too euphoric to notice. *Liz didn't look that big! Whoa.*

Rose was loaded into a humidicrib to both keep her warm and dry her out. The great cervical squeeze of the normal birthing process has the added advantage of clearing a newborn's airways of the fluid they breathe in the womb. Babies born without it tend to spit, cough and sniffle a lot, and the warm, dry air of the humidicrib helps resolve this temporary problem.

The last thing I wanted was to compromise the effectiveness of the humidicrib but I couldn't bring myself to use my camera's precious remaining memory on crap pics through plexiglass, so I had both crib portals open, one for pics of my baby's chubby face and one through which to pat her bum, although I found it hard to do both at once. It was midway through this pat-your-head-and-rub-your-tum test of coordination that Liz came wheeling into recovery next to us for a short bonding session before I was told to scrub my scrubs and become a civilian again so that I could take Rose downstairs to the nursery, where she'd spend her first night.

I reclaimed my real clothes and emerged from the change room/meat locker in record time...to find my daughter gone. This, despite assurances that this first, crucial bonding time—when (according to parenting school) children look into the eyes of their parents for the first time and electricity crackles between them— would be held sacred. I offer a daily prayer to Saint Leopold the patron saint of protracted psychological counselling that my daughter's eyes didn't open at this point and force her to mistakenly bond with Polish Anna the nursing cyclone.

It is safe to say that nurse Anna made quite an impact on us during our first night as parents.

To start with, it was definitely a faux pas for Nurse Anna to leave the operating suite with a baby and no parent. We very new parents are funny like this; we like to know where our offspring are. Call us picky, but there you have it. Luckily, when I emerged from the surgery change room to find the baby gone, there was nary a paper shoe-cover in sight to hinder my progress as I sprinted down the hallways, searching for my kidnapped daughter. Of course, with her uncanny sense of compassion Nurse Anna sensed that there was something not quite right the minute I pointedly tapped her on the shoulder, panting like a farm dog, at the door to the nursery. On the way, I'd pulled Liz's mum and aunt from the waiting room and they took up their positions at the nursery window, ready to meet the newest family member.

As a bona fide dad (still coming to grips with that term), I was given the security code to the nursery and

followed Anna and Rosie inside, where she was wheeled
in next to rows of other newborns, many of them tiny
premature babies desperately trying to struggle into the
normal weight range. In comparison, our little Rosie looked
like a bouncer at a newborn Blue Light Disco. As robust
as she was, she was still in her humidicrib with a lung
capacity sensor attached to her foot, the result displayed
in large red numbers on a readout above the crib. I'd
been told all was well when the figure stayed above 90,
and I relayed this information to her grandma and great-
aunt outside, but forgot to mention that the sensor was
prone to falling off her foot. Throughout the smiling and
waving through the nursery window the display was at
a healthy 94, until I stroked her foot a little too vigorously
and dislodged the sensor, sending the number plummeting
into the 50s. I was not too alarmed, but I was later told
there was significant distress on the other side of the
soundproof glass. If they bashed on the glass with their
fists, I didn't hear it. If we find ourselves in that position
again, I suggest that they use a chair.

After I was shown the correct way to bath my baby
without the need for tiny scuba equipment, Rosie was
wrapped up and we returned to Liz's room to be a family
for the first time. It was during this contemplative 'coming
down', bonding phase that Cyclone Anna the nurse blew
back into our room.

I am only guessing that Anna was from Poland, but
with an accent more Eastern Bloc than a nuclear meltdown
and an ID badge surname worth 500 Scrabble points,
I think it's a safe bet. Despite learning English from

the Monty Python English Phrasebook ('I will not buy this tobacconist, it is scratched') she possessed no self-consciousness in trotting out her mangled Annaspeak, talking a mile a minute with only three words in ten ringing a bell.

Just imagine yourself as a kid in your parent's Kingswood, messing with the radio dial. Remember the sound it would make when you grabbed the knob and sent the needle the length of the radio spectrum? That sound made more sense than Anna The Bedside Manner.

At the time, we had enough to deal with. Liz had a drip, a catheter, a skinful of pharmaceuticals, an angry new wound and about as much idea as me of what to do with the precious little girl gurgling in the crib/trolley beside us. But this was no concern of Anna's. She blew in and with a cheerful 'Hilla! Es ebberyun oka,' began purposefully tugging at various parts of Liz's body. By way of explanation, she continued with her patented brand of idiot-ese until Rose started fussing, Liz and I were bewildered, and I finally asked her what the hell she was playing at.

I worked out Anna wanted me to help her wrestle some sexy surgical stockings onto Liz, so we did, and my wife was soon better equipped to recover from her surgery and take advantage of any unexpected long-haul international flights that might come her way.

But Anna wasn't finished. A short course in Esperanto later, we discovered it was time for Liz's first breastfeeding session. The woman annoyed me, but I felt for Liz more. Her first attempt at breastfeeding took place with an

incomprehensible Pole tugging at her shirt, shoving pillows
under any loose limbs and insisting, 'Nip! No wur moof
da rin of dot squez of da boobie!' while she mashed Liz's
breast against Rosie's face. Four concerted beams of
daggers were fired off to no avail as Anna stayed to the
end of the feed to demonstrate how to take a common
household bunny rug and wrap a baby-shaped package
tight enough to play racquetball with.

Things got so tense that I feared Liz, despite the
catheter and drip securing her to her bed, would leap up
and strangle the woman with her (Liz's) urine tube and
leave me to stage her (Anna's) death as a freak surgical
stocking accident.

When all the nurses retreated, the blood pressure
readings were done and charts updated, we sat in the
vacuum the hubbub had left behind staring at each other
and the little girl who had just materialised, seemingly
out of nowhere. It was as if we'd just won the weekly
baby raffle at the local RSL. Two hours before, we'd been
in this very spot tapping our feet and staring at the
garden outside, and now we were parents, expected to
care for and cherish the vulnerable, beautiful little baby
that we'd dreamed about for years, gotten to know over
nine months but only just met. As Liz said later, without
the natural birthing process, there was no protracted
ordeal, no drama on which to put an exclamation mark
after the last nine months and start a new parental
sentence.

Do not get me wrong: at that moment we were more
thrilled than we could hope to express, and faced with

the significant risks of a vaginal breech birth first time around we were not about to ignore our doctor's advice, but I could see a wistful glint in Liz's eye, and I knew she would have preferred to sweat for the pot of gold at the end of the rainbow. Maybe next time.

Still, there was no arguing with the result. Now that Rose had been cleaned up we could finally take a quiet moment for a good look at our IVF miracle.

The immediate impression I got looking at Rosie was one of a robust, alert, healthy baby. Unlike both of her parents at the same age, she already had a dusting of brown hair to go with her dark blue eyes, but her eyelashes and brows were quite blonde. In some lights a reddish tinge was visible and most of her extended family would later swear she was odds-on to inherit her father's fair colouring. In other lights her father was just as confident she'd develop more olive skin like her mother. She certainly had her mother's button nose, but there was no arguing with the resemblance to my oval face and someone even detected a tiny cleft in her chin. Together with her long fingers, thumbs and limbs, it seemed many of my chromosomes had found a place in her DNA. Maybe my sperm weren't so lazy after all! As an only child who recently lost the one remaining blood relative I knew in Australia (aside from my shiny new daughter), I have never been inundated with family, so it always gives me a thrill when people say I look like one of my relatives. When people comment that they can see a lot of me (and my mum) in Rosie, I feel the need to high-five them.

Rose spent her first night out in the world in the nursery, a standard procedure for babies who have been delivered by c-section because their mothers can't move freely enough to look after them. It also gives mothers a chance to relax, recover and reflect. Occasionally, during these moments of quiet rumination on our first evening as parents, Liz would look over and say, 'Jase, you know...we've got a baby.'

I would shake my head wistfully, lean back in my chair and, in a considered manner befitting the patriarch of a young family, reply, 'Yeah. Fark.' That comment would become a theme for the rest of our hospital stay. Slowly, surely, we would gain our first spicy taste of the realities of parenthood.

Three days later the end-of-week baby boom was over and the new week brought a spacious private room. The double bed for sleepovers never eventuated, and we'd been downgraded from electric to manual, but I bravely hand-wound the bed into my favourite TV angle and the windowsill was plenty spacious enough for Liz to perch herself on. I'm kidding, of course.

Whatever kind of parent she'd make, Liz had to recover from her operation before she could do much parenting. Her first step to recovery was to lose the tubes and drips and gingerly swing down and enjoy the sensuous feel of utilitarian hospital carpet underfoot. She was sporting a six-inch scar low on her belly, but there was plenty of pain relief on hand to help her to function slowly and surely; occasional mental lapses were her main problem. With so much happening around her she would sometimes forget about her five layers of stitches and move like a normal person, producing eye-watering results. These were generally followed by a quick lie-down. But, with help from the ward nurses, visiting physios and Dr Bob, she was gradually getting back on her feet.

Rosie, on the other hand, was slowly becoming the yellow Rose of Sandgate. Opposite Rh factors in Liz's and my blood (I have A+, as does Rosie, but her mother's blood is a more pessimistic O-) flagged the fact that our little girl was likely to suffer from jaundice as her liver struggled to process any negative antibodies that might have crossed the placenta into her. Liz had a shot to combat any blood that might have gone the other way, but Rosie needed more help.

She would spend days three and four of her life back in the humidicrib, naked as the day she was born (Friday), with an elasticised Batman mask protecting her eyes from the bank of infra-red lights beating down on her. The yellow tinge had started across her button nose and was spreading across her face, and bare-skin exposure to as much ultraviolet light as possible was the answer. Quick action had to be taken to nip the problem in the bud if we had any chance of being allowed home any time before the Rapture.

I was keeping busy commuting to and from the hospital, trying to make Liz's life just that bit more comfortable by ferrying in morning hot chocolates, newspapers and scintillating commentary on how many minutes it took me to get home the previous night. She was slowly regaining the ability to get around and, what with her busy painkiller, feeding and vital signs schedule, we seemed to be flat out watching our baby get a tan.

Needless to say, Liz had it harder than me. Each day's most difficult (and often, paradoxically, most welcome) event was saying goodbye to my wife and solarium-based daughter and driving out of the hospital carpark. Somehow I was exhausted, but I had the luxury of heading home with my only commitments dog-walking, house-tidying and passing out in front of the TV. Liz, on the other hand, spent each night being woken regularly for Rosie's feeds and, although the baby was still under lights, Liz was gradually being introduced to the full burden of motherhood with the pain from her wound still impacting upon her sleep and general mobility.

Visits from friends and family were a welcome relief from the routine. During the first days of her life Rosie, when she wasn't masquerading as the world's tiniest (and most unabashedly naked) superhero, clapped eyes on her grandparents and great-grandparents regularly as they dropped in to stroke and coo at her. They'd bring cards and presents and inform us of what was happening on the 'outside', and we'd put in orders for triple-decker chocolate cakes with metal files in them.

After five days in semi-stir, we were starting to climb the walls. Liz's wound was healing well and we were dealing almost autonomously with Rosie, when she wasn't in the Las Vegas box, so why shouldn't we go home? Her yellow tinge was fading and during our last two days nurses had jabbed her heel every morning to take a blood sample to test for antibodies. Each day they'd come up with what seemed like an arbitrary figure that her reading had to be under, and each day we were closing in on it.

Eventually, on our sixth day in hospital and after a tense morning's wait for the results, Rosie's blood count passed with flying colours. I ran around doing paperwork, thanked the nurses, midwives, umpires and ball boys and, about 3pm on 4 May 2005, I loaded up the family car with my ginger wife and potentially ginger daughter and drove them home.

After almost three years, and a solitary protracted IVF cycle, our struggle to become parents had had a dream ending. As I loaded my new family into the Silver Bullet, I couldn't help but smile. I had my own little A-Team.

I love it when a plan comes together.

ROSE-COLOURED GLASSES

My dear Rosie,

A wise man once said that writing is the closest thing we have to time travel. If you're reading this, it's hard to argue with his logic. Think about it: here I am, your old dad, sitting here at a desk in a corner of the room your mum is steadily converting from an office back into a bedroom (yours, of course), speaking directly to you probably fifteen years or more in the future. Of course, if NASA and the boffins at the Ponds Institute have put their heads together to come up with space wormhole technology by the time you read this, the analogy will lose its meaning, but let's carry on regardless, shall we?

The day I write this you are exactly three weeks old. Can you believe your age was ever measured in days and weeks, rather than years? You probably can't, but at this point your mum and I find it just as hard to believe you'll eventually grow up to be the person on the other end of this inter-generational trunk call, someone capable of reading this, understanding it and being gracious enough to laugh at your dad's jokes.

Here in 2005, you are currently a little longer than my forearm and you fit perfectly into the crook of my elbow as I carry you around, from the bath to the change table to your mum's lap to your cot, which looks improbably large squeezed up beside our bed with you tucked in way down at the foot of it. That is what strikes me every time I step into the room to check on you in your bed, as I just did—you are such a tiny, vulnerable bundle surrounded by so much empty space.

Eveningwear-wise (I imagine this will be very important to you at this point, so therefore nice and embarrassing) you are wearing a white terry towelling jumpsuit, currently the staple item in your wardrobe. Convenience dictates this because they're easily undone and we need to get at your nappy quickly because MAN, can you pump out the p... Anyway, before you were born we opted for carefully gender-neutral green, yellow and white suits, but just lately your wardrobe has mysteriously turned into a sea of pink. As you will already know, your mum and I are nothing if not traditionalists, although in these enlightened times (and your times must be so enlightened that peace and love pervades the entire huperson race) boys are allowed occasional contact with that light-red colour. I am a boy and have been for some years now and even I'm getting used to all the light-red we have around. Sometimes I even select your clothes for you, although I have to wash my hands after coming into extended contact with the bad colour to protect my fragile masculinity.

You are just big enough to touch the bottom of your size triple-zero suits, but only if you stretch out and point your toes. Your mum and I got very excited last week when we discovered that you had already outgrown your size quadruple-zeros. It is a rare tangible sign that suggests you're healthy and we must be doing something right.

You see, that's the catch when you become a parent— you'll probably find out yourself one day. There is no instruction manual, and even if there was, since every baby is different (the main distinction: none are as special are yours) the booklet would end up in the recycling bin anyway. This has been evident in the hailstorm of advice we've been trekking through over the last couple of months, a storm that has intensified in the last three weeks. For every baby book available that says one settling technique is the new breakthrough in non-shrieking technology, there are three that state IN RED BLOCK LETTERS that, if you are stupid enough to leave your brain on a bus and use this technique, your baby will be irrevocably harmed, possibly even to such an extent that they end up as a member of parliament. I have also found that secret foolproof tricks touted by friends, family members and colleagues, when put into practice have the habit of inducing screams that show up on the Richter scale.

In my limited experience, there is only one pearl of wisdom that all the new books and old wives have in common: trust your instincts, and we plan to do so just as soon as we develop some. I am counting on my instinct manifesting itself as a disembodied, God-like voice that schools me on such handy subjects as *Vomit: Velocity, Trajectory, Consistency.* Sort of like a Hitchhiker's Guide To The Infancy.

I'm jealous, because your mother seems to be leaving me behind in the instinct stakes. I am part-way towards mastering the difference between your hungry face and your barf face and she is already displaying the first stage of supersonic mother hearing, easily able to pick up your softest gurgle from the other end of the house. I, on the other hand, still hear at normal levels. I know this because your mum, hanging out washing downstairs, will pick up your subsonic signals and has to generate considerable volume in her 'can you check the baby?' yell to reach me, at which point I promptly reach down and pat your bum.

The three weeks since you've joined us have been incredible. Incredible, and exhausting and mind-boggling and scary all whizzed up together in a big parental milkshake. I personally was not ready for such a big serve. My cup runneth over with tangy parenting juices.

Rose, as I've tried to convey in this book, for more than two years your mum and I thought we might not have a chance to be parents at all. It's a creeping, sickening emptiness that I hope you never have to experience, watching those around you become pregnant (some of them seemingly via overly heartfelt pecks on the cheek, or sweaty bus seats), or looking on through the media as others who have children fail to cherish them. And all the while there we were, employing teams of doctors and scientists to politely introduce our eggs and sperm in a warm, comfortable setting, complete with mood lighting and canapés. And then it's *still* touch and go whether they will do the do-se-do.

As the months turned into years and the doctors came and went, I began to lose hope of ever seeing a day when we could look down at you and see you gurgle and kick and stare up at us and put in a credible bid for the world gurning title. And every new day of not seeing you chipped away at my self-esteem.

We carried this burden for more than two years, and even though it seemed to get heavier with every new turn in the road, there are many who carry it for much longer, through many more hardships. There are still others who carry it forever. I sometimes feel embarrassed when I sit down at this little desk in your room and write about the pain and frustration that your mum and I suffered. Even though it turned into a six-month cycle, we still only had to bear one crack at IVF to be blessed with you. Clearly we have only caught a glimpse of the pain and frustration that some couples have to negotiate, and I hope we never get the full picture. It's a lesson that we would all do well to re-learn: when you feel at your lowest ebb, just remember that there is always someone worse off than you, and if they can pick themselves up and keep going, why can't you?

When I look back through the slice of my life chronicled in this book, it looks like a landscape viewed through the wrong end of a telescope. Situations I thought I just couldn't get past, let alone prevail over, now seem almost trivial. It's all about perspective. Everything looks better after a good night's sleep; time heals all wounds; a stitch in time saves two in the bush—ancient wisdom like this doesn't stand the test of time unless there's a grain of truth to it, or someone said it on *Oprah* once. Whatever their origin, these are the chestnuts I need to remember when you have been crying for three hours and I don't know why. Now you have arrived and flipped our life on its head there are new challenges that face all three of us, but that's okay. I am looking forward to them.

Rosie, I can't tell you how excited we were when you arrived. In this book I hope you've gleaned an inkling of the elation I felt when I first laid eyes on you in the delivery theatre on your very first birth day. My only fear is that I haven't done the moment justice. Suffice it to say that the ground shifted, my world changed gear and suddenly I was a new person. I looked like the old me—same utilitarian head with sandy-reddish-brown-who-the-hell-knows-what-colour hair on a not-quite-average-height frame—but mediocre arseing about suddenly wasn't going to be good enough in my life anymore. It was almost as if there is now a Jason-shaped space around me that I have to grow into to earn the right for you to call me Dad.

For the six days you were in hospital with your mum after you were born, I was all elbows, arms and wet kisses. I didn't quite know how to hold you but I couldn't keep my hands away, so there were lots of strange positions and awkward angles going on. Your mum was still off her game recovering from her caesarean section so, like a good footy team, I had the perfect chance to dominate possession. I cuddled and played and you would look at me with an old woman's quizzical gaze when I'd poke my tongue out at you or cross my eyes. When your grandma and granddad and nan and great-granddad John would visit, we'd have to form an orderly line to take turns to nurse you. If I held onto you too long the womenfolk would hover around, just slightly too polite to insist on a cuddle, but all the while pleading with their eyes.

In the hospital I once took you in my arms for a walk in the corridor outside our suite, where I was quickly told that this was not allowed. I soon slunk back into our room, but I spent the duration of our 30-second jailbreak hoping to come across nurses, visitors, any strangers to whom I could show you off. Now that I think about it, I can just conceive of the fact that maybe complete strangers wouldn't be as impressed with you as I am, but I still think it's their loss.

Your mum is just as proud of you. Even though she's exhausted from extended crying sessions and middle-of-the-night feeds, she never stops chatting, playing with and fussing over you. She talks to you like an old friend, which stands to reason. She has had an intimate relationship with you for almost ten months now, and I'm desperately playing catch-up.

To be fair, if anyone deserves a medal, it's her, although I'll take a commemorative coffee mug if you have one. Your mum has really done the hard yards since your birth, and had the majority of the medical burden to bear for a couple of years before that too, if we're keeping score. In the last three weeks, it has been she whose breasts you've chewed on around the clock, she who squeezed your cot next to our bed to keep you close enough to sacrifice sleep in return for constant contact and she who has worn the majority of your vomit, although I often also come away from a cuddle wearing chunder like war veterans wear medals. She does it because she loves and cherishes you, as do I. Despite little sleep, a painful caesarean wound and all your feeding, she is coping a shade better than me right now, although we both have had our moments, and we both have our different roles. My contribution is as chief gofer and clothes washer, and I occasionally go in to work to keep the money trickling in.

Being a dad is harder and more rewarding than I ever thought possible, and I doff my metaphorical hat to those who have done a good job in the role.

Sometimes I get so confused. The heart of the issue goes to the difference between males and females, Rose. You may do a science module of the same name in high school. Hopefully you'll pay attention rather than sniggering at all the pictures of pee-pees and girls' bits like I did. If you've read the rest of this book, you'll understand that the divergence in the sexes is far more profound than some plumbing and dangly parts.

The male of the species, as I've mentioned before, is generally a cause-and-effect kind of beast. This is especially true of me. This leads to that, tab A into slot B, step one, then two then three. These are the logical ways we chest-beating cavemen like to attack our lives. This kind of mindset has plenty of uses out here in the world, many involving inventing stuff and building tall things and then inexplicably climbing up them to leap off the top, but it's of limited value when dealing with babies. Obviously, right now when you cry you can't tell anyone what's wrong, so we primitive males are stuck with a poser—our beautiful little baby is in distress—and we have only a few known solutions to fix the problem. Once we have worked to the end of what is a very short list—mine consists of: hungry, cold, hot, nappy change, burp, tired—we first-time dads feel lost and frustrated and altogether powerless. This lost feeling is at odds with our overwhelming joy at the miracle of you, and has the potential to eat away the joy part and leave us just overwhelmed.

But another thing we blokes are good at is persevering. I love you so much and I want you to be happy and healthy so badly that I have resolved to swim at least partially against this ingrained left-brain current, which I guess is what all those other successful dads out there have done. It's time to get a little less black and white and a lot more Zen. It's those grey areas that give us blokes trouble, those miasmic, slippery pools of swirling emotions and intuition, but this is exactly the dark, disorienting place I need to explore more often. Eerily, this is exactly the same conclusion I came to after your mother and I struggled through our first year of marriage. Hmmm, what is the common element here...? Nope. Gone. Maybe it'll come to me later.

Rather than dwelling on what eludes me, here is a short list of the things I know about babies, and you specifically:

1. The first thing I know is that no-one else knows anything. People with the best intentions try to give advice, but they only know about their babies and other people's babies. Crucially, these babies are not you. In the end no-one knows more about you than your mother and me. I must remember this.

2. It's okay if we new parents don't have all the answers. The only people who expect us to are ourselves. Perverse, aren't we? If we do our best, that's all we can do, surely. Rose, don't tell anyone but I'm paraphrasing my primary school motto there. *Man* I must be old.

3. Sometimes babies just cry. This is related to the previous point. When we've done what we can to settle you but you are still upset, maybe that's okay. I guess it will have to be, eh? Let me tell you, trying to remember that goes a long way toward lowering stress levels and unknotting shoulders. We know you don't cry to spite us, and we know that you sometimes cry and no-one knows why. And that's normal.

4. You pick up on our stress. Anecdotal evidence that I have gathered in a poll of almost twelve experienced parents suggests that second babies are generally less stressed than numero unos simply because their parents are less stressed. Why? Because they've done it all before and are way past thinking that a bout of the grizzles will elicit the onset of Armageddon.

5. I told you it would be a short list.

But wait, there's more. I have also witnessed that, even though you're too young to know how to smile yet, sometimes you grin by accident (often just before a loud eruption from the pantular region, but we'll gloss over that fact) and my chest nearly bursts with joy. In the past, I had read about this bursting feeling or heard others claim to have experienced it and thought it was surely an exaggeration, a platitude dipped in saccharine and hung out there to sound good or sell greeting cards. I'd felt the odd surge of pride in the past, but nothing involving rupturing. But your smile has now set that bubble of elation expanding under my sternum, and I believe them. And I believe I want more.

I am also pretty sure that you couldn't have a more loving family, both the ones who are still around, and those you will never see in the flesh but will experience through pictures and the memories of we who knew them. And they will be with you almost as closely as we will, no matter where you are.

I doubt your mum and I would have gotten to this point had it not been for our family. It's funny to think that before I met your mother they were two completely separate groups of people, one not even aware of the other's presence on the planet, living their lives oblivious to the fact that the three of us would one day unite them so strongly. Whether they live in the cold northeast of England, Spain, in the various states of Australia, or just down the road, now they have a focal point in common—your mum and I, and now you.

To varying extents they have all been through the journey chronicled in this book, the winding path that has ended in you, my sweet little girl. Many of them crossed their fingers as we began our reproductive investigations, remained rock-like upon hearing of the dead-ends, disappointments and frustrations, and experienced true elation as they celebrated our successes with us.

Your grandmother, my mother, was our number one cheerleader and was clearly as excited as any prospective grandparent that has ever slipped down to the shops for a pair of booties. You will never meet her, Rose, but she will always be with you. If you ever want to get a sense of her, just find a mirror. As much as you and I may be peas in a pod, you resemble her just as strongly as you do me, and I suspect that this will only strengthen with time. Sometimes I think that there are reincarnative forces at work, and that you may be her back again and ready for another turn on the merry-go-round. Of course, we'll never be sure of this, but I think it's a comforting idea to play with.

I'll be interested to see whether your character bears as many similarities to her as your countenance. Your grandmother was a strong woman, a fighter, and had a tremendous capacity to adapt, change and roll with the punches. She made mistakes, as we all do, but when she was presented with an awkward wrinkle in the fabric of her life, whether it was a snag of her own doing or not, her immediate intention was to always move forward and try to become wiser from the experience. This takes some doing, especially when life throws up as many roadblocks as it seemed to do for her, and there's a silent dignity to consistently battling on that eventually leaves the ugliness of the problems you face in its wake.

There are so many things I want to tell you about her, but there are more moments to capture and foibles to chuckle over than pages available to me in this book. I'm sure I'll eventually get to them all as we grow old together (come to think of it, I'll be the one growing old, you'll just be growing) but I'll leave you with just one here. I hope it illustrates what she meant to me.

When I was much younger than you are now—I was six years old, I think—I suffered from terribly frightening dreams of falling. I've never suffered severe vertigo since, but for a short time I had a recurring dream of falling through endless blackness that would make my head spin, my ears ring and my stomach drop, even in my sleep. It was so bad that I soon became scared to go to bed at night, and when I did, I tried to stay awake at all costs. There's an old movie series called *Nightmare on Elm Street* in which this problem arises, often with madcap homicidal consequences, but I don't suggest you dig up those DVDs (or whatever light-cube technology you have there in the future) until you're a bit older. They may turn it into a self-fulfilling prophecy.

Anyway, at the time I didn't understand what was going on sufficiently to explain it properly to my mum, but the beauty of parents is that they just *know* things. All I remember of that time was my mum's vigil. She would sit on the side of my bed every night gently stroking my hair over and over for what seemed like hours, until I fell blissfully to sleep. I felt completely safe and loved and protected from the bottomless pit and any and all scar-faced psychopaths lurking under the bed. I don't recall ever having a vertigo dream while she was perched there, mesmerising me with her touch.

That's what I want to be for you, Rose. A protector and a friend and someone who just seems to know when things aren't right. Right now, we haven't known you long enough for flashes of this kind of intuition to be common, although we pick up new signs almost every day. We are just as new to parenting as you are to being out here in the world, and both of us are still feeling our way along, quickly picking up clues about how each other ticks. The main difference is that you are currently slipping in marginally more tantrums than us old folk. But give it time.

It's funny. There have been more than a few tears shed along the long road to your conception, some that I've already mentioned in this book. Many were the periods of black resignation that we, as parents-to-be, experienced after the disappointment of our latest course of ineffective drugs or unwanted period took its toll on us. It's easy to lose perspective and sink into a pit with seemingly steep sides. But then, suddenly, some good fortune provides a set of stairs and you skip out of your hole and it soon grows over. Now the happy tears are the ones I remember most. Isn't it one of the greatest aspects of human nature that the good times carry more weight than the bad.

The feeling of elation I experienced the day you were conceived was only surpassed by the indescribable emotion I encountered on the day you were born. On both occasions you can safely assume your old dad's tear ducts got a bit of a flush-out and, after years of shaking my head at womenfolk's ability to cry when they are happy, I finally got it. Several times.

Now we are a family—your mother and me, you and Bob and Matilda, and it already seems like we never existed apart.

At the moment your life (and consequently ours too) is an endless whirligig of feed-play-sleep, but I know it won't be like this forever. Soon you'll have more social engagements than soiled nappies and we'll be on to the next stage of our lives.

As I wistfully stare into the future I inevitably wonder what you are like now, as you read this. What is our life like? How old are you? You might be younger than fifteen, but surely not younger than ten. Maybe you, like me, won't develop an interest in the origins of your life and family until you are older. Maybe you won't blow the dust off this book until you are thinking about having children of your own.

As powerful as this time-warping communiqué is, it doesn't provide me with any of the answers to these questions, so I'll tell you how I imagine you now, as I sit here and type in 2005. Maybe one day we'll have a good old laugh over my bullseyes and my terrible misfires and you can rub my bald pate affectionately and call me an old duffer. I'd like that. Not the going bald part, obviously—the other bit.

Right now, I'm thinking of you reading this as a precocious teenager, full of passion and fun and with only a passing respect for authority. (This is all very well, but remember that your parents are always right. God, did I just say that?) In my mind's eye you are a tall, healthy girl with flowing auburn hair, a few freckles across a button nose, and a cheeky smile. You're sporty and excel at most that you try but, like me, you can't quite decide on one discipline. You do well at swimming and soccer—those little legs of yours pack quite a punch already—but practice takes a back seat to your art-based pursuits. There's your painting and music to attend to, and your busy social calendar on top of that, which probably consists mainly of outings with your friends to talk about boys, and outings with your friends to actively ignore boys. It's all important stuff and I look forward to teasing you mercilessly about members of my great gender. I look forward even more to testing the nerve of your boyfriends with some stern looks, gruff warnings and overbearing rumbling about. I suspect that that will

be the sport I truly excel at. I guess I think of you as
an amalgam of Pippi Longstocking, Heidi and Nikki
Webster. That's a bit strange if you think about it too
hard, so we'll move on.

I trust your smile is just as radiant and surprising as
it is here in 2005. I'm sure it will be. At the moment I
have to wait for your accidental or gas-based toothless
grins (possibly inspired by the absurdity of your parents'
crazy rushing-around antics) to bask in. With teeth your
smile will be a killer, and I'm sure by now you've learned
of its power over those around you and are trotting it
out at every opportunity. I won't mind a bit.

I wonder what colour your room is now? Today it's
a pinky-purple, and I am always careful to utter the
occasional heavily masculine affirmation if I find myself
in here for a long time. As I type, I will cry out 'trucks
are tops' or 'I am about to scratch myself in the groinular
region with some vigour' on occasion, which can scare
the dogs, but helps keep the bad colour at bay. It is
in this pink room that your change table and chest
of drawers live, together with storage cubes rapidly
overflowing with stuffed animals, mainly of the bear-
like persuasion. It is also into this pink domain that I
wheel my mum's old chopping block at bath time. It's
a large affair on a stand with wheels and on it I will
have already perched your plastic baby bath full of warm
water. We leave the main light off to get you sleepy and
I set about bathing you by the muted light of the computer
screen. We don't want you overstimulated and screaming

all night, after all. I enjoy bath time immensely and now that you are used to it you like it as much as I do.

This bathing intimacy will be unthinkable to you in your grown-up state, but it's just as unthinkable to me that you will shun me as a teenager. Here where I am I can't even conceive of what full-sized furniture you have in your room or what band posters adorn the walls in your time. Am I allowed in here anymore? Are we even living in the same house? Who knows what life has thrown at us in the last decade or more. That's what makes it such a scary and exhilarating ride.

I desperately hope you don't have any nagging issues about the technology we used to help bring you into the world, Rose. I know that in the past, when IVF and other reproductive techniques were much more rare, some children born using it later said they felt uncomfortable about it or that their parents were 'playing God'. I can't understand this reasoning, and it's increasingly rare in this time—with 3 per cent of all babies born in Australia owing their existence to this kind of medicine, kids aren't feeling so different or confused about their origins anymore. In your class at school, if all the other kids would or could lay their reproductive origins on the table, the chances are that at least one of your classmates is an IVF baby too. So how many does that make in your school? In your time I'm sure the figures are a lot higher.

If you have any doubts, Rose, just think of it like this: if you break your arm, you need medical assistance to bring the two halves of bone back together, so you accept the doctor's treatment and let nature take over and no-one bats an eyelid. Your mother and I just used IVF to bring our two genetic halves together and you grew in your mum just like every other baby born. And here you are. We still created you and the end result was the same: my sperm, your mum's egg—and you were born nine months later.

As far as playing God goes, I don't agree with the analogy, and even if I did I don't know many parents worth their Huggies who wouldn't play God if they had the chance. I think it's almost a prerequisite, caring so much that you would move Heaven and Earth to make life better (or help give life in the first place) for your children. I'd worry about parents who wouldn't at least consider this option.

Even when parents have plenty of eggs and battalions of sperm at their disposal, every child has beaten huge odds just to be conceived but, if you think about it, you have beaten even longer odds. With less sperm and fewer eggs to play with, the initial odds of your conception were longer than most. Of course, your mum and I did our best to get the medicos to lower the odds in your favour. So we enlisted some help to produce a healthy baby. That was our decision and it is no different from asking a doctor to help with a tricky delivery, in my view.

Although every child is precious, we believe you are the most precious of them all. When I was given the horrific news that I should never expect to be a father, and your mum was told that she had a condition that would make it less likely for her to produce eggs, we could have walked away with our proverbial tails between our legs, drowned our sorrows and bought another dog. But the thought of you was so precious to us that we fought tooth and nail and brought to bear all the resources we could muster to bring you into the world. This is because we knew you would be worth it.

We were right, weren't we.

For this gift, we are truly grateful, and we think it's only fair that we try to repay our karmic deficit by being the best parents we can be. You know what they say— when you have to work hard for something, you appreciate it more. Even after all the screaming, soiled pants and tantrums, I eventually calm down, change my jocks and I'm still grateful that you are here with us.

Now there's a new question to consider: will we try again? When I'm holding you during a feed, or you're cooing on the floor, I sometimes whisper in your ear to ask whether you'd like a brother or sister. You just look at me and smile. By the time you read this you will already know the answer to this question, but where I am now, it has just started to poke its head above the horizon. With such a brilliant result from our first attempt at IVF, your mother and I have already started talking about it and agree that it's a matter of *when*, not *if* we try again. As hard as the process was for us, as daunting as it seems, it is nothing compared to the joy we feel every day at you and your antics. A single smile, a glimpse of you sleeping, the memory of just one of your crazy squeals has the power to instantly erase the file of IVF stress and heartache from our memory banks.

If we need any proof that the process is a risk worth taking once more, we need only spare a thought for those parents who try fruitlessly for years. Some succeed in the end, but many don't. The rewards must be huge, if people will put themselves through this again and again, wouldn't you say?

Aside from the mother's age, there is no medical reason governing how many IVF kids parents can have, and as many go back and try again as choose to have more children naturally. This is great news, because your mother and I would dearly like a little brother or sister for you, or maybe one of each. We are both conscious that our chances will quickly diminish with time, so we are only waiting until your mum feels recovered from our first turn on the merry-go-round before we dip into the embryo freezer and try again. I was an only child and I spent much of my childhood wishing for a brother or sister to play with or tease, to beat up on or be beaten up by. If we succeed you will probably set me straight on this score one day, but I think it is important to have a sibling to share your life with. But, if we never succeed, rest assured that we are ecstatic with what we already have.

Like we did last time, we'll give our next cycle everything we've got. Who knows how it will turn out? If you want certainty, be a stop-go man. If you want fulfilment, become a dad.

Right now, it's up to us to cherish and raise you and pray that we're doing a decent job. I guess you'll let us know one day, apparently almost hourly during your teenage years. As we move forward and make a life together, all your mother and I wish for is that you grow up healthy and happy and come to respect us, and more importantly, yourself.

No-one knows what the next chapter holds, but I can't wait to see.

Love always,
Your dad.